C-1524   CAREER EXAMINATION SERIES

This is your
PASSBOOK for...

Training Technician

Test Preparation Study Guide
Questions & Answers

COPYRIGHT NOTICE

This book is SOLELY intended for, is sold ONLY to, and its use is RESTRICTED to individual, bona fide applicants or candidates who qualify by virtue of having seriously filed applications for appropriate license, certificate, professional and/or promotional advancement, higher school matriculation, scholarship, or other legitimate requirements of education and/or governmental authorities.

This book is NOT intended for use, class instruction, tutoring, training, duplication, copying, reprinting, excerption, or adaptation, etc., by:

1) Other publishers
2) Proprietors and/or Instructors of "Coaching" and/or Preparatory Courses
3) Personnel and/or Training Divisions of commercial, industrial, and governmental organizations
4) Schools, colleges, or universities and/or their departments and staffs, including teachers and other personnel
5) Testing Agencies or Bureaus
6) Study groups which seek by the purchase of a single volume to copy and/or duplicate and/or adapt this material for use by the group as a whole without having purchased individual volumes for each of the members of the group
7) Et al.

Such persons would be in violation of appropriate Federal and State statutes.

PROVISION OF LICENSING AGREEMENTS – Recognized educational, commercial, industrial, and governmental institutions and organizations, and others legitimately engaged in educational pursuits, including training, testing, and measurement activities, may address request for a licensing agreement to the copyright owners, who will determine whether, and under what conditions, including fees and charges, the materials in this book may be used them. In other words, a licensing facility exists for the legitimate use of the material in this book on other than an individual basis. However, it is asseverated and affirmed here that the material in this book CANNOT be used without the receipt of the express permission of such a licensing agreement from the Publishers. Inquiries re licensing should be addressed to the company, attention rights and permissions department.

All rights reserved, including the right of reproduction in whole or in part, in any form or by any means, electronic or mechanical, including photocopying, recording, or by any information storage and retrieval system, without permission in writing from the Publisher.

Copyright © 2025 by

National Learning Corporation

212 Michael Drive, Syosset, NY 11791
(516) 921-8888 • www.passbooks.com
E-mail: info@passbooks.com

PASSBOOK® SERIES

THE *PASSBOOK® SERIES* has been created to prepare applicants and candidates for the ultimate academic battlefield – the examination room.

At some time in our lives, each and every one of us may be required to take an examination – for validation, matriculation, admission, qualification, registration, certification, or licensure.

Based on the assumption that every applicant or candidate has met the basic formal educational standards, has taken the required number of courses, and read the necessary texts, the *PASSBOOK® SERIES* furnishes the one special preparation which may assure passing with confidence, instead of failing with insecurity. Examination questions – together with answers – are furnished as the basic vehicle for study so that the mysteries of the examination and its compounding difficulties may be eliminated or diminished by a sure method.

This book is meant to help you pass your examination provided that you qualify and are serious in your objective.

The entire field is reviewed through the huge store of content information which is succinctly presented through a provocative and challenging approach – the question-and-answer method.

A climate of success is established by furnishing the correct answers at the end of each test.

You soon learn to recognize types of questions, forms of questions, and patterns of questioning. You may even begin to anticipate expected outcomes.

You perceive that many questions are repeated or adapted so that you can gain acute insights, which may enable you to score many sure points.

You learn how to confront new questions, or types of questions, and to attack them confidently and work out the correct answers.

You note objectives and emphases, and recognize pitfalls and dangers, so that you may make positive educational adjustments.

Moreover, you are kept fully informed in relation to new concepts, methods, practices, and directions in the field.

You discover that you are actually taking the examination all the time: you are preparing for the examination by "taking" an examination, not by reading extraneous and/or supererogatory textbooks.

In short, this PASSBOOK®, used directedly, should be an important factor in helping you to pass your test.

TRAINING TECHNICIAN

JOB DUTIES
Under direction, assists with planning, development, and administration of a designated portion of the employee development training program; does other related duties as required.

EXAMPLES OF WORK
When the employee development training program has been established and approved, takes the lead in an assigned phase of training activity.
Visits several offices and subunits of the department or agency, and discusses with administrative officials their varied operating problems with a view toward training of employees.
Gives assignments and instructions to employees of the unit and othersand supervises the performance of their work.
Reviews training plans.
May assist in coordination of and oversees the conduct of training programs and may personally give orientation, inservice, refresher, and other courses.
Observes training courses and provides advice and assistance to those conducting such courses to achieve desired objectives.
Supervises and participates in preparation of procedures, schedules, training outlines, manuals, guides, and materials for implementation of the program.
Keeps current with changes in legislation and regulations, policies, and procedures which may effect department or agency programs and responsibilities and, where required, makes revisions in training courses and materials.
Keeps in touch with current literature in the field of personnel administration and employee training, and reviews training methods used by other government departments/agencies and by business and industry.
Drafts correspondence.
May prepare statistical and other reports of training matters containing findings, conclusions, and recommendations.
Supervises the maintenance of records and files.
May establish evaluation procedures to determine progress of participants and effectiveness of the training program.
May provide consultation to staff for the purpose of planning and development of training programs.
Schedules staff training programs and keeps records of participants' performance and evaluation.
Will be required to learn to utilize various types of electronic and/or manual recording and information systems used by the agency, office, or related units.

KNOWLEDGE AND ABILITIES
Knowledge of programs, responsibilities, standards, procedures, organization, rules, regulations, and administrative problems in the department or agency after a period of training.
Knowledge of and familiarity with principles, methods, tools, and techniques of personnel administration and their application in specific situations.
Knowledge of problems likely to arise in supervising studies and surveys of operating procedures and methods to determine employee deficiencies
Knowledge of principles, methods, and problems involved in planning, organization, and conducting of training courses.

Knowledge of teaching principles, methods, tools, and techniques, and their application to training programs and of the learning process.

Knowledge of principles and techniques of conducting on-the-job training.

Ability to organize assigned technical and supervisory work, analyze actual and potential training problems, and develop effective work methods.

Ability to assign, instruct, and supervise employees of the training unit.

Ability to analyze and evaluate education and training needs and in accord with such needs to evaluate and develop curricula, instructional methods, techniques, devices, and aids.

Ability to assist in the formulation of training plans and prepare training manuals and other related material.

Ability to plan and supervise the conduct of analytical studies and surveys designed to locate weakness in operating procedures and the need for employee training.

Ability to analyze and interpret basic law and regulations.

Ability to formulate tentative training plans and projects.

Ability to supervise and participate in the preparation of training outlines, manuals, and other related materials.

Ability to give advice and assistance to department or agency administrative employees concerning the need for specific kinds of employee training, approved training plans, training techniques, and the use of available training materials.

Ability to keep current with literature, trends of thought, new developments in personnel administration, and with changes in legislation which may have an effect on recruitment and the work of the department or agency and its several units, and on the utilization of employees.

Ability to establish cooperative work relationships with department or agency administrative and supervisory officials.

Ability to work harmoniously with associates, superior officials, and employees, and with those personnel interest in or concerned with inservice and other training work of the department or agency.

Ability to draft correspondence.

Ability to prepare clear, sound, accurate, arid informative statistical and other reports of training activities containing findings, conclusions, and recommendations.

Ability to supervise the maintenance of training records and files.

Ability to utilize various types of electronic and/or manual recording and information systems used by the agency, office, or related units.

Ability to read, writer speak, understand, and communicate in English sufficiently to perform duties of this position. American Sign Language or Braille may also be considered as acceptable forms of communication.

HOW TO TAKE A TEST

I. YOU MUST PASS AN EXAMINATION

A. WHAT EVERY CANDIDATE SHOULD KNOW

Examination applicants often ask us for help in preparing for the written test. What can I study in advance? What kinds of questions will be asked? How will the test be given? How will the papers be graded?

As an applicant for a civil service examination, you may be wondering about some of these things. Our purpose here is to suggest effective methods of advance study and to describe civil service examinations.

Your chances for success on this examination can be increased if you know how to prepare. Those "pre-examination jitters" can be reduced if you know what to expect. You can even experience an adventure in good citizenship if you know why civil service exams are given.

B. WHY ARE CIVIL SERVICE EXAMINATIONS GIVEN?

Civil service examinations are important to you in two ways. As a citizen, you want public jobs filled by employees who know how to do their work. As a job seeker, you want a fair chance to compete for that job on an equal footing with other candidates. The best-known means of accomplishing this two-fold goal is the competitive examination.

Exams are widely publicized throughout the nation. They may be administered for jobs in federal, state, city, municipal, town or village governments or agencies.

Any citizen may apply, with some limitations, such as the age or residence of applicants. Your experience and education may be reviewed to see whether you meet the requirements for the particular examination. When these requirements exist, they are reasonable and applied consistently to all applicants. Thus, a competitive examination may cause you some uneasiness now, but it is your privilege and safeguard.

C. HOW ARE CIVIL SERVICE EXAMS DEVELOPED?

Examinations are carefully written by trained technicians who are specialists in the field known as "psychological measurement," in consultation with recognized authorities in the field of work that the test will cover. These experts recommend the subject matter areas or skills to be tested; only those knowledges or skills important to your success on the job are included. The most reliable books and source materials available are used as references. Together, the experts and technicians judge the difficulty level of the questions.

Test technicians know how to phrase questions so that the problem is clearly stated. Their ethics do not permit "trick" or "catch" questions. Questions may have been tried out on sample groups, or subjected to statistical analysis, to determine their usefulness.

Written tests are often used in combination with performance tests, ratings of training and experience, and oral interviews. All of these measures combine to form the best-known means of finding the right person for the right job.

II. HOW TO PASS THE WRITTEN TEST

A. NATURE OF THE EXAMINATION

To prepare intelligently for civil service examinations, you should know how they differ from school examinations you have taken. In school you were assigned certain definite pages to read or subjects to cover. The examination questions were quite detailed and usually emphasized memory. Civil service exams, on the other hand, try to discover your present ability to perform the duties of a position, plus your potentiality to learn these duties. In other words, a civil service exam attempts to predict how successful you will be. Questions cover such a broad area that they cannot be as minute and detailed as school exam questions.

In the public service similar kinds of work, or positions, are grouped together in one "class." This process is known as *position-classification*. All the positions in a class are paid according to the salary range for that class. One class title covers all of these positions, and they are all tested by the same examination.

B. FOUR BASIC STEPS

1) Study the announcement

How, then, can you know what subjects to study? Our best answer is: "Learn as much as possible about the class of positions for which you've applied." The exam will test the knowledge, skills and abilities needed to do the work.

Your most valuable source of information about the position you want is the official exam announcement. This announcement lists the training and experience qualifications. Check these standards and apply only if you come reasonably close to meeting them.

The brief description of the position in the examination announcement offers some clues to the subjects which will be tested. Think about the job itself. Review the duties in your mind. Can you perform them, or are there some in which you are rusty? Fill in the blank spots in your preparation.

Many jurisdictions preview the written test in the exam announcement by including a section called "Knowledge and Abilities Required," "Scope of the Examination," or some similar heading. Here you will find out specifically what fields will be tested.

2) Review your own background

Once you learn in general what the position is all about, and what you need to know to do the work, ask yourself which subjects you already know fairly well and which need improvement. You may wonder whether to concentrate on improving your strong areas or on building some background in your fields of weakness. When the announcement has specified "some knowledge" or "considerable knowledge," or has used adjectives like "beginning principles of..." or "advanced ... methods," you can get a clue as to the number and difficulty of questions to be asked in any given field. More questions, and hence broader coverage, would be included for those subjects which are more important in the work. Now weigh your strengths and weaknesses against the job requirements and prepare accordingly.

3) Determine the level of the position

Another way to tell how intensively you should prepare is to understand the level of the job for which you are applying. Is it the entering level? In other words, is this the position in which beginners in a field of work are hired? Or is it an intermediate or advanced level? Sometimes this is indicated by such words as "Junior" or "Senior" in the class title. Other jurisdictions use Roman numerals to designate the level – Clerk I, Clerk II, for example. The word "Supervisor" sometimes appears in the title. If the level is not indicated by the title, check the description of duties. Will you be working under very close supervision, or will you have responsibility for independent decisions in this work?

4) Choose appropriate study materials

Now that you know the subjects to be examined and the relative amount of each subject to be covered, you can choose suitable study materials. For beginning level jobs, or even advanced ones, if you have a pronounced weakness in some aspect of your training, read a modern, standard textbook in that field. Be sure it is up to date and has general coverage. Such books are normally available at your library, and the librarian will be glad to help you locate one. For entry-level positions, questions of appropriate difficulty are chosen – neither highly advanced questions, nor those too simple. Such questions require careful thought but not advanced training.

If the position for which you are applying is technical or advanced, you will read more advanced, specialized material. If you are already familiar with the basic principles of your field, elementary textbooks would waste your time. Concentrate on advanced textbooks and technical periodicals. Think through the concepts and review difficult problems in your field.

These are all general sources. You can get more ideas on your own initiative, following these leads. For example, training manuals and publications of the government agency which employs workers in your field can be useful, particularly for technical and professional positions. A letter or visit to the government department involved may result in more specific study suggestions, and certainly will provide you with a more definite idea of the exact nature of the position you are seeking.

III. KINDS OF TESTS

Tests are used for purposes other than measuring knowledge and ability to perform specified duties. For some positions, it is equally important to test ability to make adjustments to new situations or to profit from training. In others, basic mental abilities not dependent on information are essential. Questions which test these things may not appear as pertinent to the duties of the position as those which test for knowledge and information. Yet they are often highly important parts of a fair examination. For very general questions, it is almost impossible to help you direct your study efforts. What we can do is to point out some of the more common of these general abilities needed in public service positions and describe some typical questions.

1) General information

Broad, general information has been found useful for predicting job success in some kinds of work. This is tested in a variety of ways, from vocabulary lists to questions about current events. Basic background in some field of work, such as sociology or economics, may be sampled in a group of questions. Often these are principles which have become familiar to most persons through exposure rather than through formal training. It is difficult to advise you how to study for these questions; being alert to the world around you is our best suggestion.

2) Verbal ability

An example of an ability needed in many positions is verbal or language ability. Verbal ability is, in brief, the ability to use and understand words. Vocabulary and grammar tests are typical measures of this ability. Reading comprehension or paragraph interpretation questions are common in many kinds of civil service tests. You are given a paragraph of written material and asked to find its central meaning.

3) Numerical ability
Number skills can be tested by the familiar arithmetic problem, by checking paired lists of numbers to see which are alike and which are different, or by interpreting charts and graphs. In the latter test, a graph may be printed in the test booklet which you are asked to use as the basis for answering questions.

4) Observation
A popular test for law-enforcement positions is the observation test. A picture is shown to you for several minutes, then taken away. Questions about the picture test your ability to observe both details and larger elements.

5) Following directions
In many positions in the public service, the employee must be able to carry out written instructions dependably and accurately. You may be given a chart with several columns, each column listing a variety of information. The questions require you to carry out directions involving the information given in the chart.

6) Skills and aptitudes
Performance tests effectively measure some manual skills and aptitudes. When the skill is one in which you are trained, such as typing or shorthand, you can practice. These tests are often very much like those given in business school or high school courses. For many of the other skills and aptitudes, however, no short-time preparation can be made. Skills and abilities natural to you or that you have developed throughout your lifetime are being tested.

Many of the general questions just described provide all the data needed to answer the questions and ask you to use your reasoning ability to find the answers. Your best preparation for these tests, as well as for tests of facts and ideas, is to be at your physical and mental best. You, no doubt, have your own methods of getting into an exam-taking mood and keeping "in shape." The next section lists some ideas on this subject.

IV. KINDS OF QUESTIONS

Only rarely is the "essay" question, which you answer in narrative form, used in civil service tests. Civil service tests are usually of the short-answer type. Full instructions for answering these questions will be given to you at the examination. But in case this is your first experience with short-answer questions and separate answer sheets, here is what you need to know:

1) Multiple-choice Questions
Most popular of the short-answer questions is the "multiple choice" or "best answer" question. It can be used, for example, to test for factual knowledge, ability to solve problems or judgment in meeting situations found at work.
A multiple-choice question is normally one of three types—
- It can begin with an incomplete statement followed by several possible endings. You are to find the one ending which *best* completes the statement, although some of the others may not be entirely wrong.
- It can also be a complete statement in the form of a question which is answered by choosing one of the statements listed.

- It can be in the form of a problem – again you select the best answer.

Here is an example of a multiple-choice question with a discussion which should give you some clues as to the method for choosing the right answer:

When an employee has a complaint about his assignment, the action which will *best* help him overcome his difficulty is to
    A. discuss his difficulty with his coworkers
    B. take the problem to the head of the organization
    C. take the problem to the person who gave him the assignment
    D. say nothing to anyone about his complaint

In answering this question, you should study each of the choices to find which is best. Consider choice "A" – Certainly an employee may discuss his complaint with fellow employees, but no change or improvement can result, and the complaint remains unresolved. Choice "B" is a poor choice since the head of the organization probably does not know what assignment you have been given, and taking your problem to him is known as "going over the head" of the supervisor. The supervisor, or person who made the assignment, is the person who can clarify it or correct any injustice. Choice "C" is, therefore, correct. To say nothing, as in choice "D," is unwise. Supervisors have and interest in knowing the problems employees are facing, and the employee is seeking a solution to his problem.

2) True/False Questions

The "true/false" or "right/wrong" form of question is sometimes used. Here a complete statement is given. Your job is to decide whether the statement is right or wrong.

SAMPLE: A roaming cell-phone call to a nearby city costs less than a non-roaming call to a distant city.

This statement is wrong, or false, since roaming calls are more expensive.
This is not a complete list of all possible question forms, although most of the others are variations of these common types. You will always get complete directions for answering questions. Be sure you understand *how* to mark your answers – ask questions until you do.

V. RECORDING YOUR ANSWERS

Computer terminals are used more and more today for many different kinds of exams.
For an examination with very few applicants, you may be told to record your answers in the test booklet itself. Separate answer sheets are much more common. If this separate answer sheet is to be scored by machine – and this is often the case – it is highly important that you mark your answers correctly in order to get credit.
An electronic scoring machine is often used in civil service offices because of the speed with which papers can be scored. Machine-scored answer sheets must be marked with a pencil, which will be given to you. This pencil has a high graphite content which responds to the electronic scoring machine. As a matter of fact, stray dots may register as answers, so do not let your pencil rest on the answer sheet while you are pondering the correct answer. Also, if your pencil lead breaks or is otherwise defective, ask for another.

Since the answer sheet will be dropped in a slot in the scoring machine, be careful not to bend the corners or get the paper crumpled.

The answer sheet normally has five vertical columns of numbers, with 30 numbers to a column. These numbers correspond to the question numbers in your test booklet. After each number, going across the page are four or five pairs of dotted lines. These short dotted lines have small letters or numbers above them. The first two pairs may also have a "T" or "F" above the letters. This indicates that the first two pairs only are to be used if the questions are of the true-false type. If the questions are multiple choice, disregard the "T" and "F" and pay attention only to the small letters or numbers.

Answer your questions in the manner of the sample that follows:

32. The largest city in the United States is
 A. Washington, D.C.
 B. New York City
 C. Chicago
 D. Detroit
 E. San Francisco

1) Choose the answer you think is best. (New York City is the largest, so "B" is correct.)
2) Find the row of dotted lines numbered the same as the question you are answering. (Find row number 32)
3) Find the pair of dotted lines corresponding to the answer. (Find the pair of lines under the mark "B.")
4) Make a solid black mark between the dotted lines.

VI. BEFORE THE TEST

Common sense will help you find procedures to follow to get ready for an examination. Too many of us, however, overlook these sensible measures. Indeed, nervousness and fatigue have been found to be the most serious reasons why applicants fail to do their best on civil service tests. Here is a list of reminders:

- Begin your preparation early – Don't wait until the last minute to go scurrying around for books and materials or to find out what the position is all about.
- Prepare continuously – An hour a night for a week is better than an all-night cram session. This has been definitely established. What is more, a night a week for a month will return better dividends than crowding your study into a shorter period of time.
- Locate the place of the exam – You have been sent a notice telling you when and where to report for the examination. If the location is in a different town or otherwise unfamiliar to you, it would be well to inquire the best route and learn something about the building.
- Relax the night before the test – Allow your mind to rest. Do not study at all that night. Plan some mild recreation or diversion; then go to bed early and get a good night's sleep.
- Get up early enough to make a leisurely trip to the place for the test – This way unforeseen events, traffic snarls, unfamiliar buildings, etc. will not upset you.
- Dress comfortably – A written test is not a fashion show. You will be known by number and not by name, so wear something comfortable.

- Leave excess paraphernalia at home – Shopping bags and odd bundles will get in your way. You need bring only the items mentioned in the official notice you received; usually everything you need is provided. Do not bring reference books to the exam. They will only confuse those last minutes and be taken away from you when in the test room.
- Arrive somewhat ahead of time – If because of transportation schedules you must get there very early, bring a newspaper or magazine to take your mind off yourself while waiting.
- Locate the examination room – When you have found the proper room, you will be directed to the seat or part of the room where you will sit. Sometimes you are given a sheet of instructions to read while you are waiting. Do not fill out any forms until you are told to do so; just read them and be prepared.
- Relax and prepare to listen to the instructions
- If you have any physical problem that may keep you from doing your best, be sure to tell the test administrator. If you are sick or in poor health, you really cannot do your best on the exam. You can come back and take the test some other time.

VII. AT THE TEST

The day of the test is here and you have the test booklet in your hand. The temptation to get going is very strong. Caution! There is more to success than knowing the right answers. You must know how to identify your papers and understand variations in the type of short-answer question used in this particular examination. Follow these suggestions for maximum results from your efforts:

1) Cooperate with the monitor
The test administrator has a duty to create a situation in which you can be as much at ease as possible. He will give instructions, tell you when to begin, check to see that you are marking your answer sheet correctly, and so on. He is not there to guard you, although he will see that your competitors do not take unfair advantage. He wants to help you do your best.

2) Listen to all instructions
Don't jump the gun! Wait until you understand all directions. In most civil service tests you get more time than you need to answer the questions. So don't be in a hurry. Read each word of instructions until you clearly understand the meaning. Study the examples, listen to all announcements and follow directions. Ask questions if you do not understand what to do.

3) Identify your papers
Civil service exams are usually identified by number only. You will be assigned a number; you must not put your name on your test papers. Be sure to copy your number correctly. Since more than one exam may be given, copy your exact examination title.

4) Plan your time
Unless you are told that a test is a "speed" or "rate of work" test, speed itself is usually not important. Time enough to answer all the questions will be provided, but this does not mean that you have all day. An overall time limit has been set. Divide the total time (in minutes) by the number of questions to determine the approximate time you have for each question.

5) Do not linger over difficult questions

If you come across a difficult question, mark it with a paper clip (useful to have along) and come back to it when you have been through the booklet. One caution if you do this – be sure to skip a number on your answer sheet as well. Check often to be sure that you have not lost your place and that you are marking in the row numbered the same as the question you are answering.

6) Read the questions

Be sure you know what the question asks! Many capable people are unsuccessful because they failed to *read* the questions correctly.

7) Answer all questions

Unless you have been instructed that a penalty will be deducted for incorrect answers, it is better to guess than to omit a question.

8) Speed tests

It is often better NOT to guess on speed tests. It has been found that on timed tests people are tempted to spend the last few seconds before time is called in marking answers at random – without even reading them – in the hope of picking up a few extra points. To discourage this practice, the instructions may warn you that your score will be "corrected" for guessing. That is, a penalty will be applied. The incorrect answers will be deducted from the correct ones, or some other penalty formula will be used.

9) Review your answers

If you finish before time is called, go back to the questions you guessed or omitted to give them further thought. Review other answers if you have time.

10) Return your test materials

If you are ready to leave before others have finished or time is called, take ALL your materials to the monitor and leave quietly. Never take any test material with you. The monitor can discover whose papers are not complete, and taking a test booklet may be grounds for disqualification.

VIII. EXAMINATION TECHNIQUES

1) Read the general instructions carefully. These are usually printed on the first page of the exam booklet. As a rule, these instructions refer to the timing of the examination; the fact that you should not start work until the signal and must stop work at a signal, etc. If there are any *special* instructions, such as a choice of questions to be answered, make sure that you note this instruction carefully.

2) When you are ready to start work on the examination, that is as soon as the signal has been given, read the instructions to each question booklet, underline any key words or phrases, such as *least, best, outline, describe* and the like. In this way you will tend to answer as requested rather than discover on reviewing your paper that you *listed without describing*, that you selected the *worst* choice rather than the *best* choice, etc.

3) If the examination is of the objective or multiple-choice type – that is, each question will also give a series of possible answers: A, B, C or D, and you are called upon to select the best answer and write the letter next to that answer on your answer paper – it is advisable to start answering each question in turn. There may be anywhere from 50 to 100 such questions in the three or four hours allotted and you can see how much time would be taken if you read through all the questions before beginning to answer any. Furthermore, if you come across a question or group of questions which you know would be difficult to answer, it would undoubtedly affect your handling of all the other questions.

4) If the examination is of the essay type and contains but a few questions, it is a moot point as to whether you should read all the questions before starting to answer any one. Of course, if you are given a choice – say five out of seven and the like – then it is essential to read all the questions so you can eliminate the two that are most difficult. If, however, you are asked to answer all the questions, there may be danger in trying to answer the easiest one first because you may find that you will spend too much time on it. The best technique is to answer the first question, then proceed to the second, etc.

5) Time your answers. Before the exam begins, write down the time it started, then add the time allowed for the examination and write down the time it must be completed, then divide the time available somewhat as follows:
    - If 3-1/2 hours are allowed, that would be 210 minutes. If you have 80 objective-type questions, that would be an average of 2-1/2 minutes per question. Allow yourself no more than 2 minutes per question, or a total of 160 minutes, which will permit about 50 minutes to review.
    - If for the time allotment of 210 minutes there are 7 essay questions to answer, that would average about 30 minutes a question. Give yourself only 25 minutes per question so that you have about 35 minutes to review.

6) The most important instruction is to *read each question* and make sure you know what is wanted. The second most important instruction is to *time yourself properly* so that you answer every question. The third most important instruction is to *answer every question*. Guess if you have to but include something for each question. Remember that you will receive no credit for a blank and will probably receive some credit if you write something in answer to an essay question. If you guess a letter – say "B" for a multiple-choice question – you may have guessed right. If you leave a blank as an answer to a multiple-choice question, the examiners may respect your feelings but it will not add a point to your score. Some exams may penalize you for wrong answers, so in such cases *only*, you may not want to guess unless you have some basis for your answer.

7) Suggestions
    a. Objective-type questions
        1. Examine the question booklet for proper sequence of pages and questions
        2. Read all instructions carefully
        3. Skip any question which seems too difficult; return to it after all other questions have been answered
        4. Apportion your time properly; do not spend too much time on any single question or group of questions

5. Note and underline key words – *all, most, fewest, least, best, worst, same, opposite,* etc.
6. Pay particular attention to negatives
7. Note unusual option, e.g., unduly long, short, complex, different or similar in content to the body of the question
8. Observe the use of "hedging" words – *probably, may, most likely,* etc.
9. Make sure that your answer is put next to the same number as the question
10. Do not second-guess unless you have good reason to believe the second answer is definitely more correct
11. Cross out original answer if you decide another answer is more accurate; do not erase until you are ready to hand your paper in
12. Answer all questions; guess unless instructed otherwise
13. Leave time for review

b. Essay questions
 1. Read each question carefully
 2. Determine exactly what is wanted. Underline key words or phrases.
 3. Decide on outline or paragraph answer
 4. Include many different points and elements unless asked to develop any one or two points or elements
 5. Show impartiality by giving pros and cons unless directed to select one side only
 6. Make and write down any assumptions you find necessary to answer the questions
 7. Watch your English, grammar, punctuation and choice of words
 8. Time your answers; don't crowd material

8) Answering the essay question

Most essay questions can be answered by framing the specific response around several key words or ideas. Here are a few such key words or ideas:

M's: manpower, materials, methods, money, management
P's: purpose, program, policy, plan, procedure, practice, problems, pitfalls, personnel, public relations

 a. Six basic steps in handling problems:
  1. Preliminary plan and background development
  2. Collect information, data and facts
  3. Analyze and interpret information, data and facts
  4. Analyze and develop solutions as well as make recommendations
  5. Prepare report and sell recommendations
  6. Install recommendations and follow up effectiveness

 b. Pitfalls to avoid
  1. *Taking things for granted* – A statement of the situation does not necessarily imply that each of the elements is necessarily true; for example, a complaint may be invalid and biased so that all that can be taken for granted is that a complaint has been registered

2. *Considering only one side of a situation* – Wherever possible, indicate several alternatives and then point out the reasons you selected the best one
3. *Failing to indicate follow up* – Whenever your answer indicates action on your part, make certain that you will take proper follow-up action to see how successful your recommendations, procedures or actions turn out to be
4. *Taking too long in answering any single question* – Remember to time your answers properly

IX. AFTER THE TEST

Scoring procedures differ in detail among civil service jurisdictions although the general principles are the same. Whether the papers are hand-scored or graded by machine we have described, they are nearly always graded by number. That is, the person who marks the paper knows only the number – never the name – of the applicant. Not until all the papers have been graded will they be matched with names. If other tests, such as training and experience or oral interview ratings have been given, scores will be combined. Different parts of the examination usually have different weights. For example, the written test might count 60 percent of the final grade, and a rating of training and experience 40 percent. In many jurisdictions, veterans will have a certain number of points added to their grades.

After the final grade has been determined, the names are placed in grade order and an eligible list is established. There are various methods for resolving ties between those who get the same final grade – probably the most common is to place first the name of the person whose application was received first. Job offers are made from the eligible list in the order the names appear on it. You will be notified of your grade and your rank as soon as all these computations have been made. This will be done as rapidly as possible.

People who are found to meet the requirements in the announcement are called "eligibles." Their names are put on a list of eligible candidates. An eligible's chances of getting a job depend on how high he stands on this list and how fast agencies are filling jobs from the list.

When a job is to be filled from a list of eligibles, the agency asks for the names of people on the list of eligibles for that job. When the civil service commission receives this request, it sends to the agency the names of the three people highest on this list. Or, if the job to be filled has specialized requirements, the office sends the agency the names of the top three persons who meet these requirements from the general list.

The appointing officer makes a choice from among the three people whose names were sent to him. If the selected person accepts the appointment, the names of the others are put back on the list to be considered for future openings.

That is the rule in hiring from all kinds of eligible lists, whether they are for typist, carpenter, chemist, or something else. For every vacancy, the appointing officer has his choice of any one of the top three eligibles on the list. This explains why the person whose name is on top of the list sometimes does not get an appointment when some of the persons lower on the list do. If the appointing officer chooses the second or third eligible, the No. 1 eligible does not get a job at once, but stays on the list until he is appointed or the list is terminated.

X. HOW TO PASS THE INTERVIEW TEST

The examination for which you applied requires an oral interview test. You have already taken the written test and you are now being called for the interview test – the final part of the formal examination.

You may think that it is not possible to prepare for an interview test and that there are no procedures to follow during an interview. Our purpose is to point out some things you can do in advance that will help you and some good rules to follow and pitfalls to avoid while you are being interviewed.

What is an interview supposed to test?

The written examination is designed to test the technical knowledge and competence of the candidate; the oral is designed to evaluate intangible qualities, not readily measured otherwise, and to establish a list showing the relative fitness of each candidate – as measured against his competitors – for the position sought. Scoring is not on the basis of "right" and "wrong," but on a sliding scale of values ranging from "not passable" to "outstanding." As a matter of fact, it is possible to achieve a relatively low score without a single "incorrect" answer because of evident weakness in the qualities being measured.

Occasionally, an examination may consist entirely of an oral test – either an individual or a group oral. In such cases, information is sought concerning the technical knowledges and abilities of the candidate, since there has been no written examination for this purpose. More commonly, however, an oral test is used to supplement a written examination.

Who conducts interviews?

The composition of oral boards varies among different jurisdictions. In nearly all, a representative of the personnel department serves as chairman. One of the members of the board may be a representative of the department in which the candidate would work. In some cases, "outside experts" are used, and, frequently, a businessman or some other representative of the general public is asked to serve. Labor and management or other special groups may be represented. The aim is to secure the services of experts in the appropriate field.

However the board is composed, it is a good idea (and not at all improper or unethical) to ascertain in advance of the interview who the members are and what groups they represent. When you are introduced to them, you will have some idea of their backgrounds and interests, and at least you will not stutter and stammer over their names.

What should be done before the interview?

While knowledge about the board members is useful and takes some of the surprise element out of the interview, there is other preparation which is more substantive. It *is* possible to prepare for an oral interview – in several ways:

1) Keep a copy of your application and review it carefully before the interview

This may be the only document before the oral board, and the starting point of the interview. Know what education and experience you have listed there, and the sequence and dates of all of it. Sometimes the board will ask you to review the highlights of your experience for them; you should not have to hem and haw doing it.

2) Study the class specification and the examination announcement

Usually, the oral board has one or both of these to guide them. The qualities, characteristics or knowledges required by the position sought are stated in these documents. They offer valuable clues as to the nature of the oral interview. For example, if the job involves supervisory responsibilities, the announcement will usually indicate that knowledge of modern supervisory methods and the qualifications of the candidate as a supervisor will be tested. If so, you can expect such questions, frequently in the form of a hypothetical situation which you are expected to solve. NEVER go into an oral without knowledge of the duties and responsibilities of the job you seek.

3) Think through each qualification required

Try to visualize the kind of questions you would ask if you were a board member. How well could you answer them? Try especially to appraise your own knowledge and background in each area, *measured against the job sought*, and identify any areas in which you are weak. Be critical and realistic – do not flatter yourself.

4) Do some general reading in areas in which you feel you may be weak

For example, if the job involves supervision and your past experience has NOT, some general reading in supervisory methods and practices, particularly in the field of human relations, might be useful. Do NOT study agency procedures or detailed manuals. The oral board will be testing your understanding and capacity, not your memory.

5) Get a good night's sleep and watch your general health and mental attitude

You will want a clear head at the interview. Take care of a cold or any other minor ailment, and of course, no hangovers.

What should be done on the day of the interview?

Now comes the day of the interview itself. Give yourself plenty of time to get there. Plan to arrive somewhat ahead of the scheduled time, particularly if your appointment is in the fore part of the day. If a previous candidate fails to appear, the board might be ready for you a bit early. By early afternoon an oral board is almost invariably behind schedule if there are many candidates, and you may have to wait. Take along a book or magazine to read, or your application to review, but leave any extraneous material in the waiting room when you go in for your interview. In any event, relax and compose yourself.

The matter of dress is important. The board is forming impressions about you – from your experience, your manners, your attitude, and your appearance. Give your personal appearance careful attention. Dress your best, but not your flashiest. Choose conservative, appropriate clothing, and be sure it is immaculate. This is a business interview, and your appearance should indicate that you regard it as such. Besides, being well groomed and properly dressed will help boost your confidence.

Sooner or later, someone will call your name and escort you into the interview room. *This is it.* From here on you are on your own. It is too late for any more preparation. But remember, you asked for this opportunity to prove your fitness, and you are here because your request was granted.

What happens when you go in?

The usual sequence of events will be as follows: The clerk (who is often the board stenographer) will introduce you to the chairman of the oral board, who will introduce you to the other members of the board. Acknowledge the introductions before you sit down. Do not be surprised if you find a microphone facing you or a stenotypist sitting by. Oral interviews are usually recorded in the event of an appeal or other review.

Usually the chairman of the board will open the interview by reviewing the highlights of your education and work experience from your application – primarily for the benefit of the other members of the board, as well as to get the material into the record. Do not interrupt or comment unless there is an error or significant misinterpretation; if that is the case, do not hesitate. But do not quibble about insignificant matters. Also, he will usually ask you some question about your education, experience or your present job – partly to get you to start talking and to establish the interviewing "rapport." He may start the actual questioning, or turn it over to one of the other members. Frequently, each member undertakes the questioning on a particular area, one in which he is perhaps most competent, so you can expect each member to participate in the examination. Because time is limited, you may also expect some rather abrupt switches in the direction the questioning takes, so do not be upset by it. Normally, a board member will not pursue a single line of questioning unless he discovers a particular strength or weakness.

After each member has participated, the chairman will usually ask whether any member has any further questions, then will ask you if you have anything you wish to add. Unless you are expecting this question, it may floor you. Worse, it may start you off on an extended, extemporaneous speech. The board is not usually seeking more information. The question is principally to offer you a last opportunity to present further qualifications or to indicate that you have nothing to add. So, if you feel that a significant qualification or characteristic has been overlooked, it is proper to point it out in a sentence or so. Do not compliment the board on the thoroughness of their examination – they have been sketchy, and you know it. If you wish, merely say, "No thank you, I have nothing further to add." This is a point where you can "talk yourself out" of a good impression or fail to present an important bit of information. Remember, *you close the interview yourself.*

The chairman will then say, "That is all, Mr. _____, thank you." Do not be startled; the interview is over, and quicker than you think. Thank him, gather your belongings and take your leave. Save your sigh of relief for the other side of the door.

How to put your best foot forward

Throughout this entire process, you may feel that the board individually and collectively is trying to pierce your defenses, seek out your hidden weaknesses and embarrass and confuse you. Actually, this is not true. They are obliged to make an appraisal of your qualifications for the job you are seeking, and they want to see you in your best light. Remember, they must interview all candidates and a non-cooperative candidate may become a failure in spite of their best efforts to bring out his qualifications. Here are 15 suggestions that will help you:

1) Be natural – Keep your attitude confident, not cocky

If you are not confident that you can do the job, do not expect the board to be. Do not apologize for your weaknesses, try to bring out your strong points. The board is interested in a positive, not negative, presentation. Cockiness will antagonize any board member and make him wonder if you are covering up a weakness by a false show of strength.

2) Get comfortable, but don't lounge or sprawl

Sit erectly but not stiffly. A careless posture may lead the board to conclude that you are careless in other things, or at least that you are not impressed by the importance of the occasion. Either conclusion is natural, even if incorrect. Do not fuss with your clothing, a pencil or an ashtray. Your hands may occasionally be useful to emphasize a point; do not let them become a point of distraction.

3) Do not wisecrack or make small talk

This is a serious situation, and your attitude should show that you consider it as such. Further, the time of the board is limited – they do not want to waste it, and neither should you.

4) Do not exaggerate your experience or abilities
In the first place, from information in the application or other interviews and sources, the board may know more about you than you think. Secondly, you probably will not get away with it. An experienced board is rather adept at spotting such a situation, so do not take the chance.

5) If you know a board member, do not make a point of it, yet do not hide it
Certainly you are not fooling him, and probably not the other members of the board. Do not try to take advantage of your acquaintanceship – it will probably do you little good.

6) Do not dominate the interview
Let the board do that. They will give you the clues – do not assume that you have to do all the talking. Realize that the board has a number of questions to ask you, and do not try to take up all the interview time by showing off your extensive knowledge of the answer to the first one.

7) Be attentive
You only have 20 minutes or so, and you should keep your attention at its sharpest throughout. When a member is addressing a problem or question to you, give him your undivided attention. Address your reply principally to him, but do not exclude the other board members.

8) Do not interrupt
A board member may be stating a problem for you to analyze. He will ask you a question when the time comes. Let him state the problem, and wait for the question.

9) Make sure you understand the question
Do not try to answer until you are sure what the question is. If it is not clear, restate it in your own words or ask the board member to clarify it for you. However, do not haggle about minor elements.

10) Reply promptly but not hastily
A common entry on oral board rating sheets is "candidate responded readily," or "candidate hesitated in replies." Respond as promptly and quickly as you can, but do not jump to a hasty, ill-considered answer.

11) Do not be peremptory in your answers
A brief answer is proper – but do not fire your answer back. That is a losing game from your point of view. The board member can probably ask questions much faster than you can answer them.

12) Do not try to create the answer you think the board member wants
He is interested in what kind of mind you have and how it works – not in playing games. Furthermore, he can usually spot this practice and will actually grade you down on it.

13) Do not switch sides in your reply merely to agree with a board member
Frequently, a member will take a contrary position merely to draw you out and to see if you are willing and able to defend your point of view. Do not start a debate, yet do not surrender a good position. If a position is worth taking, it is worth defending.

14) Do not be afraid to admit an error in judgment if you are shown to be wrong

The board knows that you are forced to reply without any opportunity for careful consideration. Your answer may be demonstrably wrong. If so, admit it and get on with the interview.

15) Do not dwell at length on your present job

The opening question may relate to your present assignment. Answer the question but do not go into an extended discussion. You are being examined for a *new* job, not your present one. As a matter of fact, try to phrase ALL your answers in terms of the job for which you are being examined.

Basis of Rating

Probably you will forget most of these "do's" and "don'ts" when you walk into the oral interview room. Even remembering them all will not ensure you a passing grade. Perhaps you did not have the qualifications in the first place. But remembering them will help you to put your best foot forward, without treading on the toes of the board members.

Rumor and popular opinion to the contrary notwithstanding, an oral board wants you to make the best appearance possible. They know you are under pressure – but they also want to see how you respond to it as a guide to what your reaction would be under the pressures of the job you seek. They will be influenced by the degree of poise you display, the personal traits you show and the manner in which you respond.

ABOUT THIS BOOK

This book contains tests divided into Examination Sections. Go through each test, answering every question in the margin. We have also attached a sample answer sheet at the back of the book that can be removed and used. At the end of each test look at the answer key and check your answers. On the ones you got wrong, look at the right answer choice and learn. Do not fill in the answers first. Do not memorize the questions and answers, but understand the answer and principles involved. On your test, the questions will likely be different from the samples. Questions are changed and new ones added. If you understand these past questions you should have success with any changes that arise. Tests may consist of several types of questions. We have additional books on each subject should more study be advisable or necessary for you. Finally, the more you study, the better prepared you will be. This book is intended to be the last thing you study before you walk into the examination room. Prior study of relevant texts is also recommended. NLC publishes some of these in our Fundamental Series. Knowledge and good sense are important factors in passing your exam. Good luck also helps. So now study this Passbook, absorb the material contained within and take that knowledge into the examination. Then do your best to pass that exam.

EXAMINATION SECTION

EXAMINATION SECTION
TEST 1

DIRECTIONS: Each question or incomplete statement is followed by several suggested answers or completions. Select the one that BEST answers the question or completes the statement. *PRINT THE LETTER OF THE CORRECT ANSWER IN THE SPACE AT THE RIGHT.*

1. The one of the following which is the CHIEF reason for the difference between the administration of justice agencies and that of other units in public administration is that
   A. correctional institutions are concerned with security
   B. some defendants are proven to be innocent after trial
   C. the administration of justice is more complicated than other aspects of public administration
   D. correctional institutions produce services their clients or customers fail to understand or ask for

1.____

2. Of the following, the MOST important reason why employees resist change is that
   A. they have not received adequate training in preparation for the change
   B. experience has shown that when new ideas don't work, employees get blamed and not the individuals responsible for the new ideas
   C. new ideas and methods almost always represent a threat to the security of the individuals involved
   D. new ideas often are not practical and disrupt operations unnecessarily

2.____

3. Stress situations are ideal for building up a backlog of knowledge about an employee's behavior. Not only does it inform the supervisor of many aspects of a person's behavior patterns, but it is also vitally important to have foreknowledge of how people behave under stress.
   The one of the following which is NOT implied by this passage is that
   A. a person under stress may give some indication of his unsuitability for work in an institution
   B. putting people under stress is the best means of determining their usual patterns of behavior
   C. stress situations may give important clues about performance in the service
   D. there is a need to know about a person's reaction to situations *when the chips are down*

3.____

4. There are situations requiring a supervisor to give direct orders to subordinates assigned to work under the direct control of other supervisors.
   Under which of the following conditions would this shift of command responsibility be MOST appropriate?
   A. Emergency operations require the cooperative action of two or more organizational units.

4.____

B. One of the other supervisors is not doing his job, thus defeating the goals of the organization.
C. The subordinates are performing their assigned tasks in the absence of their own supervisor.
D. The subordinates ask a superior officer who is not their own supervisor how to perform an assignment given them by their supervisor.

5. The one of the following which BEST differentiates staff supervision from line supervision is that
   A. staff supervision has the authority to immediately correct a line subordinate's action
   B. staff supervision is an advisory relationship
   C. line supervision goes beyond the normal boundaries of direct supervision within a command
   D. line supervision does not report findings and make recommendations

6. Decision-making is a rational process calling for a *suspended judgment* by the supervisor until all the facts have been ascertained and analyzed, and the consequences of alternative courses of action studied; then the decision maker
   A. acts as both judge and jury and selects what he believes to be the best of the alternative plans
   B. consults with those who will be most directly involved to obtain a recommendation as to the most appropriate course of action
   C. reviews the facts which he has already analyzed, reduces his thoughts to writing, and selects that course of action which can have the fewest negative consequences if his thinking contains an error
   D. stops, considers the matter for at least a 24-hour period, before referring it to a superior for evaluation

7. Decision-making can be defined as the
   A. delegation of authority and responsibility to persons capable of performing their assigned duties with moderate or little supervision
   B. imposition of a supervisor's decision upon a work group
   C. technique of selecting the course of action with the most desired consequences, and the least undesired or unexpected consequence
   D. process principally concerned with improvement of procedures

8. A supervisor who is not well-motivated and has no desire to accept basic responsibilities will
   A. compromise to the extent of permitting poor performance for lengthy periods without correction
   B. get good performance from his work group if the employees are satisfied with their pay and other working conditions
   C. not have marginal workers in his work group if the work is interesting
   D. perform adequately as long as the work of his group consists of routine operations

9. A supervisor is more than a bond or connecting link between two levels of employees. He has joint responsibility which must be shared with both management and with the work group.
Of the following, the item which BEST expresses the meaning of this statement is:
   A. A supervisor works with both management and the work group and must reconcile the differences between them.
   B. In management, the supervisor is solely concerned with efforts directing the work of his subordinates.
   C. The supervisory role is basically that of a liaison man between management and the work force.
   D. What a supervisor says and does when confronted with day-to-day problems depends upon is level in the organization.

9.____

10. Operations research is the observation of operations in business or government, and it utilizes both hypotheses and controlled experiments to determine the outcome of decisions. In effect, it reproduces the future impact on the decision in a clinical environment suited to intensive study.
Operations research has
   A. been more promising than applied research in the ascertaining of knowledge for the purpose of decision-making
   B. never been amenable to fact analysis on the grand scale
   C. not been used extensively in government
   D. proven to be the only rational and logical approach to decision-making on long-range problems

10.____

11. Assume that a civilian makes a complaint regarding the behavior of a certain worker to the supervisor of the worker. The supervisor regards the complaint as unjustified and unreasonable.
In this circumstances, the supervisor
   A. must make a written note of the complaint and forward it through channels to the unit or individual responsible for complaint investigations
   B. should assure the complainant that disciplinary action will be appropriate to the seriousness of the alleged offense
   C. should immediately summon the worker if he is available so that the latter may attempt to straighten out the difficulty
   D. should inform the complainant that his complaint appears to be unjustified and unreasonable

11.____

12. Modern management usually establishes a personal history folder for an employee at the time of hiring. Disciplinary matters appear in such personal history folders. Employees do not like the idea of disciplinary actions appearing in their permanent personal folders.
Authorities believe that
   A. after a few years have passed since the commission of the infraction, disciplinary actions should be removed from folders
   B. disciplinary actions should remain in folders; it is not the records but the use of records that requires detailed study

12.____

C. most personnel have not had disciplinary action taken against them and would resent the removal of disciplinary actions for such folders
D. there is no point in removing disciplinary actions from personal history folders since employees who have been guilty of infractions should not be allowed to forget their infractions

13. While supervisors should not fear the acceptance of responsibility, they
    A. generally seek out responsibility that subordinates should exercise, particularly when the supervisors do not have sufficient work to do
    B. must be on guard against the abuse of authority that often accompanies the acceptance of total responsibility
    C. should avoid responsibility that is customarily exercised by their superiors
    D. who are anxious for promotions accept responsibility but do not exercise the authority warranted by the responsibility

13._____

14. Planning is part of the decision-making process. By planning is meant the development of details of alternative plans of action.
The key to *effective* planning is
    A. careful research to determine whether a tentative plan has been tried at some time in the past
    B. participation by employees in planning, preferably those employees who will be involved in putting the selected plan into action
    C. speed; poor plans can be discarded after they are put into effect while good plans usually are not put into effect because of delays
    D. writing the plan up in considerable detail and then forwarding the plan, through channels, to the executive officer having final approval of the plan

14._____

15. Equating strict discipline with punitive measures and lax discipline with rehabilitation creates a false dichotomy.
The one of the statements given below that would BEST follow from the belief expressed in this statement is that discipline
    A. is important for treatment
    B. militates against treatment programs
    C. is not an important consideration in institutions where effective rehabilitation programs prevail
    D. minimizes the need for punitive measures if it is strict

15._____

16. If training starts at the lower level of command, it is like planting a seed in tilled ground but removing the sun and rain. Seeds cannot grow unless they have help from above.
Of the following, the MOST appropriate conclusion to be drawn from this statement is that
    A. the head of an institution may not delegate authority for the planning of an institutional training program for staff
    B. on-the-job training is better than formalized training courses
    C. regularly scheduled training courses must be planned in advance
    D. staff training is the responsibility of higher levels of comman

16._____

17. The one of the following that BEST describes the meaning of *in-service staff training* is:
    A. The training of personnel who are below average in performance
    B. The training given to each employee throughout his employment
    C. The training of staff only in their own specialized fields
    D. Classroom training where the instructor and employees develop a positive and productive relationship leading to improved efficiency on the job

17.____

18. All bureau personnel should be concerned about, and involved in, public relations.
    Of the following, the MOST important reason for this statement is that
    A. an institution is an agency of the government supported by public funds and responsible to the public
    B. institutions are places of public business and, therefore, the public is interested in them
    C. some personnel need publicity in order to advance
    D. personnel sometimes need publicity in order to ensure that their grievances are acted upon by higher authority

18.____

19. The MOST important factor in establishing a disciplinary policy in an organization is
    A. consistency of application   B. strict supervisors
    C. strong enforcement   D. the degree of toughness or laxity

19.____

20. The FIRST step in planning a program is to
    A. clearly define the objectives   B. estimate the costs
    C. hire a program director   D. solicit funds

20.____

21. The PRIMARY purpose of control in an organization is to
    A. punish those who do not do their job well
    B. get people to do what is necessary to achieve an objective
    C. develop clearly stated rules and regulations
    D. regulate expenditures

21.____

22. The UNDERLYING principle of *sound* administration is to
    A. base administration on investigation of facts
    B. have plenty of resources available
    C. hire a strong administrator
    D. establish a broad policy

22.____

23. An IMPORTANT aspect to keep in mind during the decision-making process is that
    A. all possible alternatives for attaining goals should be sought out and considered
    B. considering various alternatives only leads to confusion
    C. once a decision has been made, it cannot be retracted
    D. there is only one correct method to reach any goal

23.____

24. Implementation of accountability requires
    A. a leader who will not hesitate to take punitive action
    B. an established system of communication from the bottom to the top
    C. explicit directives from leaders
    D. too much expense to justify it

25. The CHIEF danger of a decentralized control system is that
    A. excessive reports and communications will be generated
    B. problem areas may not be detected readily
    C. the expense will become prohibitive
    D. this will result in too many *chiefs*

KEY (CORRECT ANSWERS)

1.	D		11.	D
2.	C		12.	A
3.	B		13.	B
4.	A		14.	B
5.	B		15.	A
6.	A		16.	D
7.	C		17.	B
8.	A		18.	A
9.	A		19.	A
10.	C		20.	A

21.	B
22.	A
23.	A
24.	B
25.	B

TEST 2

DIRECTIONS: Each question or incomplete statement is followed by several suggested answers or completions. Select the one that BEST answers the question or completes the statement. *PRINT THE LETTER OF THE CORRECT ANSWER IN THE SPACE AT THE RIGHT.*

1. When giving orders to his subordinates, a certain supervisor often includes information as to why the work is necessary.
   This approach by the supervisor is GENERALLY
   A. *inadvisable*, since it appears that he is avoiding responsibility and wishes to blame his superiors
   B. *inadvisable*, since it creates the impression that he is trying to impress the subordinates with his importance
   C. *advisable*, since it serves to motivate the subordinates by giving them a reason for wanting to do the work
   D. *advisable*, since it shows that he is knowledgeable and is in control of his assignments

   1.____

2. Some supervisors often ask capable, professional subordinates to get some work done with questions such as: *Mary, would you try to complete that work today?*
   The use of such request orders USUALLY
   A. gets results which are as good as or better than results from direct orders
   B. shows the supervisor to be weak and lowers the respect of his subordinates
   C. provokes resentment as compared to the use of direct orders
   D. leads to confusion as to the proper procedure to follow when carrying out orders

   2.____

3. Assume that a supervisor, because of an emergency when time was essential, and in the absence of his immediate superior, went out of the chain of command to get a decision from a higher level.
   It would consequently be MOST appropriate for the immediate superior to
   A. reprimand him for his action, since the long-range consequences are far more detrimental than the immediate gain
   B. encourage him to use this method, since the chain of command is an outmoded and discredited system which inhibits productive work
   C. order him to refrain from any repetition of this action in the future
   D. support him as long as he informed the superior of the action at the earliest opportunity

   3.____

4. A supervisor gave instructions which he knew were somewhat complex to a subordinate. He then asked the subordinate to repeat the instructions to him.
   The supervisor's decision to have the subordinate repeat the instructions was
   A. *good practice*, mainly because the subordinate would realize the importance of carefully following instructions

   4.____

7

B. *poor practice*, mainly because the supervisor should have given the employee time to ponder the instructions, and then, if necessary, to ask questions
C. *good practice*, mainly because the supervisor could see whether the subordinate had any apparent problem in understanding the instructions
D. *poor practice*, mainly because the subordinate should not be expected to have the same degree of knowledge as the supervisor

5. Supervisors and subordinates must successfully communicate with each other in order to work well together.
Which of the following statements concerning communication of this type is CORRECT?
   A. When speaking to his subordinates, a supervisor should make every effort to appear knowledgeable about all aspects of their work.
   B. Written communications should be prepared by the supervisor at his own level of comprehension.
   C. The average employee tends to give meaning to communication according to his personal interpretation.
   D. The effective supervisor communicates as much information as he has available to anyone who is interested.

6. A supervisor should be aware of situations in which it is helpful to put his orders to his subordinates in writing.
Which of the following situations would MOST likely call for a written order rather than an oral order?
The order
   A. gives complicated instructions which vary from ordinary practice
   B. involves the performance of duties for which the subordinate is responsible
   C. directs subordinates to perform duties similar to those which they performed in the recent past
   D. concerns a matter that must be promptly completed or dealt with

7. Assume that a supervisor discovers that a false rumor about possible layoffs has spread among his subordinates through the grapevine.
Of the following, the BEST way for the supervisor to deal with this situation is to
   A. use the grapevine to leak accurate information
   B. call a meeting to provide information and to answer questions
   C. post a notice on the bulletin board denying the rumor
   D. institute procedures designed to eliminate the grapevine

8. Communications in an organization with many levels becomes subject to different interpretations at each level and have a tendency to become distorted. The more levels there are in an organization, the greater the likelihood that the final recipient of a communication will get the wrong message.
The one of the following statements which BEST supports the foregoing viewpoint is:
   A. Substantial communications problems exist at high management levels in organizations.

B. There is a relationship in an organization between the number of hierarchical levels and interference with communications.
C. An opportunity should be given to subordinates at all levels to communicate their views with impunity.
D. In larger organizations, there tends to be more interference with downward communications than with upward communications.

9. A subordinate comes to you, his supervisor, to ask a detailed question about a new agency directive; however, you do not know the answer.
Of the following, the MOST helpful response to give the subordinate is to
    A. point out that since your own supervisor has failed to keep you informed of this matter, it is probably unimportant
    B. give the most logical interpretation you can, based on your best judgment
    C. ask him to raise the question with other supervisors until he finds one who knows the answer, then let you know also
    D. explain that you do not know and assure him that you will get the information for him

9._____

10. The traditional view of management theory is that communication in an organization should follow the table of organization. A newer theory holds that timely communication often requires bypassing certain steps in the hierarchical chain.
However, the MAIN advantage of using formal channels of communication within an organization is that
    A. an employee is thereby restricted in his relationships to his immediate superior and his immediate subordinates
    B. information is thereby transmitted to everyone who should be informed
    C. the organization will have an appeal channel, or a mechanism by which subordinates can go over their superior's head
    D. employees are thereby encouraged to exercise individual initiative

10._____

11. It is unfair to hold subordinates responsible for the performance of duties for which they do not have the requisite authority.
When this is done, it violates the principle that
    A. responsibility cannot be greater than that implied by delegated authority
    B. responsibility should be greater than that implied by delegated authority
    C. authority cannot be greater than that implied by delegated responsibility
    D. authority should be greater than that implied by delegated responsibility

11._____

12. Assume that a supervisor wishes to delegate some tasks to a capable subordinate.
It would be MOST in keeping with the principles of delegation for the supervisor to
    A. ask another supervisor who is experienced in the delegated tasks to evaluate the subordinate's work from time to time
    B. monitor continually the subordinate's performance by carefully reviewing his work

12._____

C. request experienced employees to submit peer ratings of the work of the subordinate
D. tell the subordinates what problems are likely to be encountered and specify which problems to report on

13. There are three types of leadership: *autocratic*, in which the leader makes the decisions and seeks compliance from his subordinates; *democratic*, in which the leader consults with his subordinate and lets them help set policy; and *free rein*, in which the leader acts as an information center and exercises minimum control over his subordinates.
A supervisor can be MOST effective if he decides to
    A. use democratic leadership techniques exclusively
    B. avoid the use of autocratic leadership techniques entirely
    C. employ the three types of leadership according to the situation
    D. rely mainly on autocratic leadership techniques

13.____

14. During a busy period of work, Employee A asked his supervisor for leave in order to take an ordinary vacation. The supervisor denied the request. The following day, Employee B asked for leave during the same period because his wife had just gone to the hospital for an indeterminate stay and he had family matters to tend to.
Of the following, the BEST way for the supervisor to deal with Employee B's request is to
    A. grant the request and give the reason to the other employee
    B. suggest that the employee make his request to higher management
    C. delay the request immediately since granting it would show favoritism
    D. defer any decision until the duration of the hospital stay is determined

14.____

15. Assume that you are a supervisor and that a subordinate tells you he has a grievance.
In general, you should FIRST
    A. move the grievance forward in order to get a prompt decision
    B. discourage this type of behavior on the part of subordinates
    C. attempt to settle the grievance
    D. refer the subordinate to the personnel office

15.____

16. A supervisor may have available a large variety of rewards he can use to motivate his subordinates. However, some supervisors choose the wrong rewards.
A supervisor is MOST likely to make such a mistake if he
    A. appeals to a subordinate's desire to be well regarded by his co-workers
    B. assumes that the subordinate's goals and preferences are the same as his own
    C. conducts in-depth discussions with a subordinate in order to discover his preference
    D. limits incentives to those rewards which he is authorized to provide or to recommend

16.____

5 (#2)

17. Employee performance appraisal is open to many kinds of errors.
When a supervisor is preparing such an appraisal, he is MOST likely to commit an error if
    A. employees are indifferent to the consequences of their performance appraisals
    B. the entire period for which the evaluation is being made is taken into consideration
    C. standard measurement criteria are used as performance benchmarks
    D. personal characteristics of employees which are not job-related are given weight

17.____

18. Assume that a supervisor finds that a report prepared by an employee is unsatisfactory and should be done over.
Which of the following should the supervisor do?
    A. Give the report to another employee who can complete it properly
    B. Have the report done over by the same employee after successfully training him
    C. Hold a meeting to train all the employees so as not to single out the employee who performed unsatisfactory
    D. Accept the report so as not to discourage the employee and then make the corrections himself

18.____

19. Employees sometimes wish to have personal advice and counseling, in confidence, about their job-related problems. These problems may include such concerns as health matters, family difficulties, alcoholism, debts, emotional disturbances, etc.
Such assistance is BEST provided through
    A. maintenance of an exit interview program to find reasons for, and solutions to, turn-over problems
    B. arrangements for employees to discuss individual problems informally outside normal administrative channels
    C. procedures which allow employees to submit anonymous inquiries to the personnel department
    D. special hearing committees consisting of top management in addition to immediate supervisors

19.____

20. An employee is always a member of some unit of the formal organization.
He may also be a member of an informal work group.
With respect to employee productivity and job satisfaction, the informal work group can MOST accurately be said to
    A. have no influence of any kind on its members
    B. influence its members negatively only
    C. influence its members positively only
    D. influence its members negatively or positively

20.____

21. In order to encourage employees to make suggestions, many public agencies have employee suggestion programs.
What is the MAJOR benefit of such a program to the agency as a whole?

21.____

It
- A. brings existing or future problems to management's attention
- B. reduces the number of minor accidents
- C. requires employees to share in decision-making responsibilities
- D. reveals employees who have inadequate job knowledge

22. Assume that you have been asked to interview a seemingly shy applicant for a temporary position in your department.
For you to ask the kinds of questions that begin with *What, Where, Why, When, Who, and How,* is
    - A. *good practice*; it informs the applicant that he must conform to the requirements of the department
    - B. *poor practice*; it exceeds the extent and purpose of an initial interview
    - C. *good practice*; it encourages the applicant to talk to a greater extent
    - D. *poor practice*; it encourages the applicant to dominate the discussion

23. In recent years, job enlargement or job enrichment has tended to replace job simplification.
Those who advocate job enrichment or enlargement consider it *desirable* CHIEFLY because
    - A. it allows supervisors to control closely the activities of subordinates
    - B. it produces greater job satisfaction through reduction of responsibility
    - C. most employees prefer to avoid work which is new and challenging
    - D. positions with routinized duties are unlikely to provide job satisfaction

24. Job rotation is a training method in which an employee temporarily changes places with another employee of equal rank.
What is usually the MAIN purpose of job rotation? To
    - A. politely remove the person being rotated from an unsuitable assignment
    - B. increase skills and provide broader experience
    - C. prepare the person being rotated for a permanent change
    - D. test the skills of the person being rotated

25. There are several principles that a supervisor needs to know if he is to deal adequately with his training responsibilities.
Which of the following is usually NOT a principle of training?
    - A. People should be trained according to their individual needs.
    - B. People can learn by being told or shown how to do work but best of all by doing work under guidance.
    - C. People can be easily trained even if they have no desire to learn.
    - D. Training should be planned, scheduled, executed, and evaluated systematically.

KEY (CORRECT ANSWERS)

1.	C		11.	A
2.	A		12.	D
3.	D		13.	C
4.	C		14.	A
5.	C		15.	C
6.	A		16.	B
7.	B		17.	D
8.	B		18.	B
9.	D		19.	B
10.	B		20.	D

21. A
22. C
23. D
24. B
25. C

EXAMINATION SECTION
TEST 1

DIRECTIONS: Each question or incomplete statement is followed by several suggested answers or completions. Select the one that BEST answers the question or completes the statement. *PRINT THE LETTER OF THE CORRECT ANSWER IN THE SPACE AT THE RIGHT.*

1. Although some kinds of instructions are best put in written form, a supervisor can give many instructions verbally.
   In which one of the following situations would verbal instructions be MOST suitable?
   A. Furnishing an employee with the details to be checked in doing a certain job
   B. Instructing an employee on the changes necessary to update the office manual used in your unit
   C. Informing a new employee where different kinds of supplies and equipment that he might need are kept
   D. Presenting an assignment to an employee who will be held accountable for following a series of steps

    1.____

2. You may be asked to evaluate the organization structure of your unit.
   Which one of the following questions would you NOT expect to take up in an evaluation of this kind?
   A. Is there an employee whose personal problems are interfering with his or her work?
   B. Is there an up-to-date job description for each position in this section?
   C. Are related operations and tasks grouped together and regularly assigned together?
   D. Are responsibilities divided as far as possible, and is this division clearly understood by all employees?

    2.____

3. In order to distribute and schedule work fairly and efficiently, a supervisor may wish to make a work distribution study. A simple way of getting the information necessary for such a study is to have everyone for one week keep track of each task doe and the time spent on each.
   Which one of the following situations showing up in such study would MOST clearly call for corrective action?
   A. The newest employee takes longer to do most tasks than do experienced employees.
   B. One difficult operation takes longer to do than most other operations carried out by the section.
   C. A particular employee is very frequently assigned tasks that are not similar and have no relationship to each other.
   D. The most highly skilled employee is often assigned the most difficult jobs.

    3.____

4. The authority to carry out a job can be delegated to a subordinate, but the supervisor remains responsible for the work of the section as a whole.
As a supervisor, which of the following rules would be the BEST one for you to follow in view of the above statement?
   A. Avoid assigning important tasks to your subordinates, because you will be blamed if anything goes wrong
   B. Be sure each subordinate understands the specific job he has been assigned, and check at intervals to make sure assignments are done properly
   C. Assign several people to every important job so that responsibility will be spread out as much as possible
   D. Have an experienced subordinate check all work done by other employees so that there will be little chance of anything going wrong

5. The human tendency to resist change is often reflected in higher rates of turnover, absenteeism, and errors whenever an important change is made in an organization. Although psychologists do not fully understand the reasons why people resist change, they believe that the resistance stems from a threat to the individual's security, that it is a form of fear of the unknown.
In light of this statement, which one of the following approaches would probably be MOST effective in preparing employees for a change in procedure in their unit?
   A. Avoid letting employees know anything about the change until the last possible moment
   B. Sympathize with employees who resent the change and let them know you share their doubts and fears
   C. Promise the employees that if the change turns out to be a poor one, you will allow them to suggest a return to the old system
   D. Make sure that employees know the reasons for the change and are aware of the benefits that are expected from it

6. Each of the following methods of encouraging employee participation in work planning has been used effectively with different kinds and sizes of employee groups.
Which one of the following methods would be MOST suitable for a group of four technically skilled employees?
   A. Discussions between the supervisor and a representative of the group
   B. A suggestion program with semi-annual awards for outstanding suggestions
   C. A group discussion summoned whenever a major problem remains unsolved for more than a month
   D. Day-to-day exchange of information, opinions, and experience

7. Of the following, the MOST important reason why a supervisor is given the authority to tell subordinates what work they should do, how they should do it, and when it should be done is that usually
   A. most people will not work unless there is someone with authority standing over them

B. work is accomplished more effectively if the supervisor plans and coordinates it
C. when division of work is left up to subordinates, there is constant arguing, and very little work is accomplished
D. subordinates are not familiar with the tasks to be performed

8. Fatigue is a factor that affects productivity in all work situations. However, a brief rest period will ordinarily serve to restore a person from fatigue.
According to this statement, which one of the following techniques is MOST likely to reduce the impact of fatigue on overall productivity in a unit?
   A. Scheduling several short breaks throughout the day
   B. Allowing employees to go home early
   C. Extending the lunch period an extra half hour
   D. Rotating job assignments every few weeks

9. After giving a new task to an employee, it is a good idea for a supervisor to ask specific questions to make sure that the employee grasps the essentials of the task and sees how it can be carried out. Questions which ask the employee what he thinks or how he feels about an important aspect of the task are particularly effective.
Which one of the following questions is NOT the type of question which would be useful in the foregoing situation?
   A. Do you feel there will be any trouble meeting the 4:30 deadline?
   B. How do you feel about the kind of work we do here?
   C. Do you think that combining those two steps will work all right?
   D. Can you think of any additional equipment you may need for this process?

10. Of the following, the LEAST important reason for having a *continuous* training program is that
    A. employees may forget procedures that they have already learned
    B. employees may develop shortcuts on the job that result in inaccurate work
    C. the job continue to change because of new procedures and equipment
    D. training is one means of measuring effectiveness and productivity on the job

11. In training a new employee, it is usually advisable to break down the job into meaningful parts and have the new employee master one part before going on to the next.
Of the following, the BEST reason for using this technique is to
    A. let the new employee know the reason for what he is doing and thus encourage him to remain in the unit
    B. make the employee aware of the importance of the work and encourage him to work harder
    C. show the employee that the work is easy so that he will be encouraged to work faster
    D. make it more likely that the employee will experience success and will be encouraged to continue learning the job

12. You may occasionally find a serious error in the work of one of your subordinates.
    Of the following, the BEST time to discuss such an error with an employee usually is
    A. immediately after the error is found
    B. after about two weeks, since you will also be able to point out some good things that the employee has accomplished
    C. when you have discovered a pattern of errors on the part of this employee so that he will not be able to dispute your criticism
    D. after the error results in a complaint by your own supervisor

13. For very important announcements to the staff, a supervisor should usually use both written and oral communications. For example, when a new procedure is to be introduced, the supervisor can more easily obtain the group's acceptance by giving his subordinates a rough draft of the new procedure and calling a meeting of all his subordinates.
    The LEAST important benefit of this technique is that it will better enable the supervisor to
    A. explain why the change is necessary
    B. make adjustments in the new procedure to meet valid staff objections
    C. assign someone to carry out the new procedure
    D. answer questions about the new procedure

14. Assume that, while you are interviewing an individual to obtain information, the individual pauses in the middle of an answer.
    The BEST of the following actions for you to take at that time is to
    A. correct any inaccuracies in what he has said
    B. remain silent until he continues
    C. explain your position on the matter being discussed
    D. explain that time is short and that he must complete his story quickly

15. When you are interviewing someone to obtain information, the BEST of the following reasons for you to repeat certain of his exact words is to
    A. assure him that appropriate action will be taken
    B. encourage him to switch to another topic of discussion
    C. assure him that you agree with his point of view
    D. encourage him to elaborate on a point he has made

16. Generally, when writing a letter, the use of precise words and concise sentences is
    A. *good*, because less time will be required to write the letter
    B. *bad*, because it is most likely that the reader will think the letter is unimportant and will not respond favorably
    C. *good*, because it is likely that your desired meaning will be conveyed to the reader
    D. *bad*, because your letter will be too brief to provide adequate information

17. In which of the following cases would it be MOST desirable to have two cards for one individual in a single alphabetic file?
    The individual has
    A. a hyphenated surname
    B. two middle names
    C. a first name with an unusual spelling
    D. a compound first name

18. Of the following, it is MOST appropriate to use a form letter when it is necessary to answer many
    A. requests or inquiries from a single individual
    B. follow-up letters from individuals requesting additional information
    C. request or inquiries about a single subject
    D. complaints from individuals that they have been unable to obtain various types of information

19. Assume that you are asked to make up a budget for your section for the coming year, and you are told that the most important function of the budget is its "control function."
    Of the following, "control" in this context implies MOST NEARLY that
    A. you will probably be asked to justify expenditures in any category when it looks as though these expenditures are departing greatly from the amount budgeted
    B. your section will probably not be allowed to spend more than the budgeted amount in any given category, although it is always permissible to spend less
    C. your section will be required to spend the exact amount budgeted in every category
    D. the budget will be filed in the Office of the Comptroller so that when a year is over the actual expenditures can be compared with the amounts in the budget

20. In writing a report, the practice of taking up the LEAST important points *first* and the most important points *last* is a
    A. *good* technique, since the final points made in a report will make the greatest impression on the reader
    B. *good* technique, since the material is presented in a more logical manner and will lead directly to the conclusions
    C. *poor* technique, since the reader's time is wasted by having to review irrelevant information before finishing the report
    D. *poor* technique, since it may cause the reader to lose interest in the report and arrive at incorrect conclusions about the report

21. Typically, when the technique of "supervision by results" is practiced, higher management sets down, either implicitly or explicitly, certain performance standards or goals that the subordinate is expected to meet. So long as these standards are met, management interferes very little.
    The MOST likely result of the use of this technique is that it will

A. lead to ambiguity in terms of goals
B. be successful only to the extent that close direct supervision is practiced
C. make it possible to evaluate both employee and supervisory effectiveness
D. allow for complete dependence on the subordinate's part

22. When making written evaluations and reviews of the performance of subordinates, it is usually ADVISABLE to
    A. avoid informing the employee of the evaluation if it is critical because it may create hard feelings
    B. avoid informing the employee of the evaluation whether critical or favorable because it is tension-producing
    C. to permit the employee to see the evaluation but not to discuss it with him because the supervisor cannot be certain where the discussion might lead
    D. to discuss the evaluation openly with the employee because it helps the employee understand what is expected of him

22._____

23. There are a number of well-known and respected human relations principles that successful supervisors have been using for years in building good relationships with their employees.
    Which of the following does NOT illustrate such a principle?
    A. Give clear and complete instructions
    B. Let each person know how he is getting along
    C. Keep an open-door policy
    D. Make all relationships personal ones

23._____

24. Assume that it is necessary for you to give an unpleasant assignment to one of your subordinates. You expect this employee to raise some objections to this assignment.
    The MOST appropriate of the following actions for you to take FIRST is to issue the assignment
    A. *orally*, with the further statement that you will not listen to any complaints
    B. *in writing*, to forestall any complaints by the employee
    C. *orally*, permitting the employee to express his feelings
    D. *in writing*, with a note that any comments should be submitted in writing

24._____

25. Suppose you have just announced at a staff meeting with your subordinates that a radical reorganization of work will take place next week. Your subordinates at the meeting appear to be excited, tense, and worried.
    Of the following, the BEST action for you to take at that time is to
    A. schedule private conferences with each subordinate to obtain his reaction to the meeting
    B. close the meeting and tell your subordinates to return immediately to their work assignments
    C. give your subordinates some time to ask questions and discuss your announcement
    D. insist that your subordinates do not discuss your announcement among themselves or with other members of the agency

25._____

KEY (CORRECT ANSWERS)

1.	C	11.	D
2.	A	12.	A
3.	C	13.	C
4.	B	14.	B
5.	D	15.	D
6.	D	16.	C
7.	B	17.	A
8.	A	18.	C
9.	B	19.	A
10.	D	20.	D

21. C
22. D
23. D
24. C
25. C

TEST 2

DIRECTIONS: Each question or incomplete statement is followed by several suggested answers or completions. Select the one that BEST answers the question or completes the statement. *PRINT THE LETTER OF THE CORRECT ANSWER IN THE SPACE AT THE RIGHT.*

1. Of the following, the BEST way for a supervisor to increase employees' interest in their work is to
    A. allow them to make as many decisions as possible
    B. demonstrate to them that he is as technically competent as they
    C. give each employee a difficult assignment
    D. promptly convey to them instructions from higher management

    1.____

2. The one of the following which is LEAST important in maintaining a high level of productivity on the part of employees is the
    A. provision of optimum physical working conditions for employees
    B. strength of employees' aspirations for promotion
    C. anticipated satisfactions which employees hope to derive from their work
    D. employees' interest in their jobs

    2.____

3. Of the following, the MAJOR advantage of group problem-solving, as compared to individual problem-solving, is that groups will more readily
    A. abide by their own decisions
    B. agree with agency management
    C. devise new policies and procedures
    D. reach conclusions sooner

    3.____

4. The group problem-solving conference is a useful supervisory method for getting people to reach solutions to problems.
    Of the following, the reason that groups usually reach more realistic solutions than do individuals is that
    A. individuals, as a rule, take longer than do groups in reaching decisions and are, therefore, more likely to make an error
    B. bringing people together to let them confer impresses participants with the seriousness of problems
    C. groups are generally more concerned with the future in evaluating organizational problems
    D. the erroneous opinions of group members tend to be corrected by the other members

    4.____

5. A competent supervisor should be able to distinguish between human and technical problems.
    Of the following, the MAJOR difference between such problems is that serious human problems, in comparison to ordinary technical problems
    A. are remedied more quickly
    B. involve a lesser need for diagnosis
    C. are more difficult to define
    D. become known through indications which are usually the actual problem

    5.____

6. Of the following, the BEST justification for a public agency establishing an alcoholism program for its employees is that
    A. alcoholism has traditionally been looked upon with a certain amused tolerance by management and thereby ignored as a serious illness
    B. employees with drinking problems have twice as many on-the-job accidents, especially during the early years of the problem
    C. excessive use of alcohol is associated with personality instability hindering informal social relationships among peers and subordinates
    D. the agency's public reputation will suffer despite an employee's drinking problem being a personal matter of little public concern

7. Assume you are a manager and you find a group of maintenance employees assigned to your project drinking and playing cards for money in an incinerator room after their regular working hours.
   The one of the following actions it would be BEST for you to take is to
    A. suspend all employees immediately if there is no question in your mind as to the validity of the charges
    B. review the personnel records of those involved with the supervisor and make a joint decision on which employees should sustain penalties of loss of annual leave or fines
    C. ask the supervisor to interview each violator and submit written reports to you and thereafter consult with the supervisor about disciplinary actions
    D. deduct three days of annual leave from each employee involved if he pleads guilty in lieu of facing more serious charges

8. Assume that as a manager you must discipline a subordinate, but all of the pertinent facts necessary for a full determination of the appropriate action to take are not yet available. However, you fear that a delay in disciplinary action may damage the morale of other employees.
   The one of the following which is MOST appropriate for you to do in this matter is to
    A. take immediate disciplinary action as if all the pertinent facts were available
    B. wait until all pertinent facts are available before reaching a decision
    C. inform the subordinate that you know he is guilty, issue a stern warning, and then let him wait for your further action
    D. reduce the severity of the discipline appropriate for the violation

9. There are two standard dismissal procedures utilized by most public agencies. The first is the "open back door" policy, in which the decision of a supervisor in discharging an employee for reasons of inefficiency cannot be cancelled by the central personnel agency. The second is the "closed back door" policy, in which the central personnel agency can order the supervisor to restore the discharged employee to his position.
   Of the following, the major DISADVANTAGE of the "closed back door" policy as opposed to the "open back door" policy is that central personnel agencies are
    A. likely to approve the dismissal of employees when there is inadequate justification

B. likely to revoke dismissal actions out of sympathy for employees
C. less qualified than employing agencies to evaluate the efficiency of employees
D. easily influenced by political, religious, and racial factors

10. The one of the following for which a formal grievance-handling system is LEAST useful is in
    A. reducing the frequency of employee complaints
    B. diminishing the likelihood of arbitrary action by supervisors
    C. providing an outlet for employee frustrations
    D. bringing employee problems to the attention of higher management

11. The one of the following managers whose leadership style involves the GREATEST delegation of authority to subordinates is the one who presents to subordinates
    A. his ideas and invites questions
    B. his decision and persuades them to accept it
    C. the problem, gets their suggestions, and makes his decision
    D. a tentative decision which is subject to change

12. Which of the following is MOST likely to cause employee productivity standards to be set too high?
    A. Standards of productivity are set by first-line supervisors rather than by higher level managers.
    B. Employees' opinions about productivity standards are sought through written questionnaires.
    C. Initial studies concerning productivity are conducted by staff specialists.
    D. Ideal work conditions assumed in the productivity standards are lacking in actual operations.

13. The one of the following which states the MAIN value of an organization chart for a manager is that such charts show the
    A. lines of formal authority
    B. manner in which duties are performed by each employee
    C. flow of work among employees on the same level
    D. specific responsibilities of each position

14. Which of the following BEST names the usual role of a line unit with regard to the organization's programs?
    A. Seeking publicity   B. Developing
    C. Carrying out   D. Evaluating

15. Critics of promotion *from within* a public agency argue for hiring *from outside* the agency because they believe that promotion from within leads to
    A. resentment and consequent weakened morale on the part of those not promoted
    B. the perpetuation of outdated practices and policies
    C. a more complex hiring procedure than hiring from outside the agency
    D. problems of objectively appraising someone already in the organization

10.____

11.____

12.____

13.____

14.____

15.____

16. The one of the following management functions which usually can be handled MOST effectively by a committee is the
    A. settlement of interdepartmental disputes
    B. planning of routine work schedules
    C. dissemination of information
    D. assignment of personnel

    16.____

17. Assume that you are serving on a committee which is considering proposals in order to recommend a new maintenance policy. After eliminating a number of proposals by unanimous consent, the committee is deadlocked on three proposals.
    The one of the following which is the BEST way for the committee to reach agreement on a proposal they could recommend is to
    A. consider and vote on each proposal separately by secret ballot
    B. examine and discuss the three proposals until the proponents of two of them are persuaded they are wrong
    C. reach a synthesis which incorporates the significant features of each proposals
    D. discuss the three proposals until the proponents of each one concede those aspects of the proposals about which there is disagreement

    17.____

18. A commonly used training and development method for professional staff is the case method, which utilizes the description of a situation, real or simulated, to provide a common base for analysis, discussion, and problem-solving.
    Of the following, the MOST appropriate time to use the case method is when professional staff needs
    A. insight into their personality problems
    B. practice in applying management concepts to their own problems
    C. practical experience in the assignment of delegated responsibilities
    D. to know how to function in many different capacities

    18.____

19. The incident process is a training and development method in which trainees are given a very brief statement of an event or o a situation presenting a job incident or an employee problem of special significance.
    Of the following, it is MOST appropriate to use the incident process when
    A. trainees need to learn to review and analyze facts before solving a problem
    B. there are a large number of trainees who require the same information
    C. there are too many trainees to carry on effective discussion
    D. trainees are not aware of the effect of their behavior on others

    19.____

20. The one of the following types of information about which a clerical employee is usually LEAST concerned during the orientation process is
    A. his specific job duties   B. where he will work
    C. his organization's history   D. who his associates will be

    20.____

21. The one of the following which is the MOST important limitation on the degree to which work should be broken down into specialized tasks is the point at which
    A. there ceases to be sufficient work of a specialized nature to occupy employees
    B. training costs equal the half-yearly savings derived from further specialization
    C. supervision of employees performing specialized tasks becomes more technical than supervision of general employees
    D. it becomes more difficult to replace the specialist than to replace the generalist who performs a complex set of functions

22. When a supervisor is asked for his opinion of the suitability for promotion of a subordinate, the supervisor is actually being asked to predict the subordinate's future behavior in a new role.
    Such a prediction is MOST likely to be accurate if the
    A. higher position is similar to the subordinate's current one
    B. higher position requires intangible personal qualities
    C. new position has had little personal association with the subordinate away from the job

23. In one form of the non-directive evaluation interview, the supervisor communicates his evaluation to the employee and then listens to the employee's response without making further suggestions.
    The one of the following which is the PRINCIPAL danger of this method of evaluation is that the employee is MOST likely to
    A. develop an indifferent attitude towards the supervisor
    B. fail to discover ways of improving his performance
    C. become resistant to change in the organization's structure
    D. place the blame for his shortcomings on his co-workers

24. In establishing rules for his subordinates, a superior should be PRIMARILY concerned with
    A. creating sufficient flexibility to allow for exceptions
    B. making employees aware of the reasons for the rules and the penalties for infractions
    C. establishing the strength of his own position in relation to his subordinates
    D. having his subordinates know that such rules will be imposed in a personal manner

25. The practice of conducting staff training sessions on a periodic basis is generally considered
    A. *poor*; it takes employees away from their work assignments
    B. *poor*; all staff training should be done on an individual basis
    C. *good*; it permits the regular introduction of new methods and techniques
    D. *good*; it ensures a high employee productivity rate

KEY (CORRECT ANSWERS)

1. A
2. A
3. A
4. D
5. C

6. B
7. C
8. B
9. C
10. A

11. C
12. D
13. A
14. C
15. B

16. A
17. C
18. B
19. A
20. C

21. A
22. A
23. B
24. B
25. C

EXAMINATION SECTION
TEST 1

DIRECTIONS: Each question or incomplete statement is followed by several suggested answers or completions. Select the one that BEST answers the question or completes the statement. *PRINT THE LETTER OF THE CORRECT ANSWER IN THE SPACE AT THE RIGHT.*

1. Following are three statements concerning on-the-job training: 1.____
   I. On-the-job training is rarely used as a method of training employees.
   II. On-the-job training is often carried on with little or no planning.
   III. On-the-job training is often less expensive than other types.
   Which of the following BEST classifies the above statements into those that are correct and those that are not?
      A. I is correct, but II and III are not.   B. II is correct but I and III are not.
      C. I and II are correct, but III is not.   D. II and III are correct, but I is not.

2. The one of the following which is NOT a valid principle for a supervisor to keep 2.____
   in mind when talking to a subordinate about his performance is:
      A. People frequently know when they deserve criticism.
      B. Supervisors should be prepared to offer suggestions to subordinates about how to improve their work.
      C. Good points should be discussed before bad points.
      D. Magnifying a subordinate's faults will get him to improve faster.

3. In many organizations information travels quickly through the grapevine. 3.____
   Following are three statements concerning the *grapevine*:
   I. Information a subordinate does not want to tell her supervisor may reach the supervisor through the *grapevine*.
   II. A supervisor can often do her job better by knowing the information that travels through the *grapevine*.
   III. A supervisor can depend on the *grapevine* as a way to get accurate information from the employees on his staff.
   Which one of the following CORRECTLY classifies the above statements into those which are generally correct and those which are not?
      A. II is correct, but I and III are not.   B. III is correct, but I and II are not.
      C. I and II are correct, but III is not.   D. I and III are correct, but II is not.

4. Following are three statements concerning supervision: 4.____
   I. A supervisor knows he is doing a good job if his subordinates depend upon him to make every decision.
   II. A supervisor who delegates authority to his subordinates soon finds that his subordinates begin to resent him.
   III. Giving credit for good work is frequently an effective method of getting subordinates to work harder

Which one of the following CORRECTLY classifies the above statements into those that are correct and those that are not?
- A. I and II are correct, but III is not.
- B. II and III are correct, but I is not.
- C. II is correct, but I and III are not.
- D. III is correct, but I and II are not.

5. Of the following, the LEAST appropriate action for a supervisor to take in preparing a disciplinary case against a subordinate is to
   - A. keep careful records of each incident in which the subordinate has been guilty of misconduct or incompetency, even though immediate disciplinary action may not be necessary
   - B. discuss with the employee each incident of misconduct as it occurs so the employee knows where he stands
   - C. accept memoranda from any other employees who may have been witnesses to acts of misconduct
   - D. keep the subordinate's personnel file confidential so that he is unaware of the evidence being gathered against him

6. Praise by a supervisor can be an important element in motivating subordinates. Following are three statements concerning a supervisor's praise of subordinates:
   I. In order to be effective, praise must be lavish and constantly restated.
   II. Praise should be given in a manner which meets the needs of the individual subordinate.
   III. The subordinate whose work is praised should believe that the praise is earned.

   Which of the following CORRECTLY classifies the above statements into those that are correct and those that are not?
   - A. I is correct, but II and III are not.
   - B. II and III are correct, but I is not.
   - C. III is correct, but I and II are not.
   - D. I and II are correct, but III is not.

7. A supervisor feels that he is about to lose his temper while reprimanding a subordinate.
   Of the following, the BEST action for the supervisor to take is to
   - A. postpone the reprimand for a short time until his self-control is assured
   - B. continue the reprimand because a loss of temper by the supervisor will show the subordinate the seriousness of the error he made
   - C. continue the reprimand because failure to do so will show that the supervisor does not have complete self-control
   - D. postpone the reprimand until the subordinate is capable of understanding the reason for the supervisor's loss of temper

8. Following are three statements concerning various ways of giving orders to subordinates:
   I. An implied order or suggestion is usually appropriate for the inexperienced employee.
   II. A polite request is less likely to upset a sensitive subordinate than a direct order.
   III. A direct order is usually appropriate in an emergency situation.

Which of the following CORRECTLY classifies the above statements into those that are correct and those that are not?
- A. I is correct, but II and III are not.
- B. II and III are correct, but I is not.
- C. III is correct, but I and II are not.
- D. I and II are correct, but III is not.

9. The one of the following which is NOT an acceptable reason for taking disciplinary action against a subordinate guilty of serious violations of the rules is that
    - A. the supervisor can *let off steam* against subordinates who break rules frequently
    - B. a subordinate whose work continues to be unsatisfactory may be terminated
    - C. a subordinate may be encouraged to improve his work
    - D. an example is set for other employees

10. At the first meeting with your staff after appointment as a supervisor, you find considerable indifference and some hostility among the participants.
    Of the following, the MOST appropriate way to handle this situation is to
    - A. disregard the attitudes displayed and continue to make your presentation until you have completed it
    - B. discontinue your presentation but continue the meeting and attempt to find out the reasons for their attitudes
    - C. warm up your audience with some good-natured statements and anecdotes and then proceed with your presentation
    - D. discontinue the meeting and set up personal interviews with the staff members to try to find out the reason for their attitude

11. Use a written rather than oral communication to amend any previous written communication.
    Of the following, the BEST justification for this statement is that
    - A. oral changes will be considered more impersonal and thus less important
    - B. oral changes will be forgotten or recalled indifferently
    - C. written communications are clearer and shorter
    - D. written communications are better able to convey feeling tone

12. Assume that a certain supervisor, when writing important communications to his subordinates, often repeats certain points in different words.
    This technique is GENERALLY
    - A. *ineffective*; it tends to confuse rather than help
    - B. *effective*; it tends to improve understanding by the subordinates
    - C. *ineffective*; it unnecessarily increases the length of the communication and may annoy the subordinates
    - D. *effective*; repetition is always an advantage in communications

13. In preparing a letter or a report, a supervisor may wish to persuade the reader of the correctness of some idea or course of action.
    The BEST way to accomplish this is for the supervisor to
    - A. encourage the reader to make a prompt decision
    - B. express each idea in a separate paragraph

C. present the subject matter of the letter in the first paragraph
D. state the potential benefits for the reader

14. Effective communications, a basic necessity for successful supervision is a two-way street. A good supervisor needs to listen to, as well as disseminate, information and he must be able to encourage his subordinates to communicate with him.
Which of the following suggestions will contribute LEAST to improving the *listening power* of a supervisor?
    A. Don't assume anything; don't anticipate, and don't let a subordinate think you know what he is going to say
    B. Don't interrupt; let him have his full say even if it requires a second session that day to get the full story
    C. React quickly to his statements so that he knows you are interested, even if you must draw some conclusions prematurely
    D. Try to understand the real need for his talking to you even if it is quite different from the subject under discussion

15. Of the following, the MOST useful approach for the supervisor to take toward the informal employee communications network known as the *grapevine* is to
    A. remain isolated from it, but not take any active steps to eliminate it
    B. listen to it, but not depend on it for accurate information
    C. use it to disseminate confidential information
    D. eliminate it as diplomatically as possible

16. If a supervisor is asked to estimate the number of employees that he believes he will need in his unit in the coming fiscal year, the supervisor should FIRST attempt to learn the
    A. nature and size of the workload his unit will have during that time
    B. cost of hiring and training new employees
    C. average number of employee absences per year
    D. number of employees needed to indirectly support or assist his unit

17. An important supervisory responsibility is coordinating the operations of the unit. This may include setting work schedules, controlling work quality, establishing interim due dates, etc. In order to handle this task, it has been divided into the following five stages:
    I. Determine the steps or sequence required for the tasks to be performed.
    II. Give the orders, either written or oral, to begin work on the tasks.
    III. Check up by following each task to make sure it is proceeding according to plan.
    IV. Schedule the jobs by setting a time for each task of operation to begin and end.
    V. Control the process by correcting conditions which interfere with the plan.
    The MOST logical sequence in which these planning steps should be performed is:
    A. I, II, III, IV, V   B. II, I, V, III, IV   C. I, IV, II, III, V   D. IV, I, II, III, V

18. Assume that a supervisor calls a meeting with the staff under his supervision in order to discuss several proposals. After some discussion, he realizes that he strongly disagrees with one proposal that four of the staff have rather firmly favored.
    At this point, he could BEST handle the situation by saying:
    A. *I have the responsibility for this decision, and I must disagree.*
    B. *I am just reminding you that I have had a great deal more experience in these matters.*
    C. *You have presented some good points, but perhaps we could look at it another way.*
    D. *The only way that this proposal can be disposed of is to defer it for further discussion.*

19. As far as the social activities and groups of his subordinates are concerned, a supervisor in a large organization can BEST strengthen his tools of leadership by
    A. emphasizing the organization as a whole and forbidding the formation of groups
    B. ignoring the groups as much as possible and dealing with each subordinate as an individual
    C. learning about the status structure of employee groups and their values
    D. avoiding any relationship with groups

20. If a subordinate asks you, his superior, for advice in planning his career in the department, you should
    A. encourage him to feel that he can easily reach the top of his occupational ladder
    B. discourage him from setting his hopes too high
    C. discuss career opportunities realistically with him
    D. explain that you have no control over his opportunities for advancement

21. A supervisor's evaluation of an employee is usually based upon a combination of objective facts and subjective judgments or opinions.
    Which of the following aspects of an employee's work or performance is MOST likely to be subjectively evaluated?
    A. Quantity   B. Accuracy   C. Attitude   D. Attendance

22. Of the following possible characteristics of supervisors, the one MOST likely to lead to failure as a supervisor is
    A. a tendency to seek several opinions before making decisions in complex matters
    B. lack of a strong desire to advance to a top position in management
    C. little formal training in human relations skills
    D. poor relations with subordinates and other supervisory personnel

23. People who break rules do so for a number of reasons. However, employees will break rules LESS often if
    A. the supervisor uses his own judgment about work methods
    B. the supervisor pretends to act strictly, but isn't really serious about it
    C. they greatly enjoy their work
    D. they have completed many years of service

24. Assume that an employee under your supervision has become resentful and generally non-cooperative after his request for transfer to another office closer to his place of residence was denied. The request was denied primarily because of the importance of his current assignment. The employee has been a valued worker, but you are now worried that his resentful attitude will have a detrimental effect.
    Of the following, the MOST desirable way for you to handle this situation is to
    A. arrange for the employee's transfer to the office he originally requested
    B. arrange for the employee's transfer to another office, but not the one he originally requested
    C. attempt to re-focus the employee's attention on those aspects of his current assignment which will be most rewarding and satisfying to him
    D. explain to the employee that, while you are sympathetic to his request, department rules will not allow transfers for reasons of personal convenience

25. Of the following, it would be LEAST advisable for a supervisor to use his administrative authority to affect the behavior and activities of his subordinates when he is trying to
    A. change the way his subordinates perform a particular task
    B. establish a minimum level of conformity to established rules
    C. bring about change in the attitudes of his subordinates
    D. improve the speed with which his subordinates respond to his orders

26. Assume that a supervisor gives his subordinate instructions which are appropriate and clear. The subordinate thereupon refuses to follow these instructions.
    Of the following, it would then be MOST appropriate for the supervisor to
    A. attempt to find out what it is that the employee objects to
    B. take disciplinary action that same day
    C. remind the subordinate about supervisory authority and threaten him with discipline
    D. insist that the subordinate carry out the order immediately

27. Of the following, the MOST effective way to identify training needs resulting from gradual changes in procedure is to
    A. monitor on a continuous basis the actual jobs performed and the skills required
    B. periodically send out a written questionnaire asking personnel to identify their needs
    C. conduct interviews at regular intervals with selected employees
    D. consult employees' personnel records

28. Assume that you, as a supervisor, have had a new employee assigned to you. If the duties of his position can be broken into independent parts, which of the following is usually the BEST way to train this new employee?
Start with
    A. the easiest duties and progressively proceed to the most difficult
    B. something easy; move to something difficult; then back to something easy
    C. something difficult; move to something easy; then to something difficult
    D. the most difficult duties and progressively proceed to the easiest

29. The oldest and most commonly used training technique is on-the-job training. Instruction is given to the worker by his supervisor or by another employee. Such training is essential in most jobs, although it is not always effective when used alone.
This technique, however, can be effectively used alone if
    A. the skills involved can be learned quickly
    B. a large number of people are to be trained at one time
    C. other forms of training have not been previously used with the people involved
    D. the skills to be taught are mental rather than manual

30. It is generally agreed that the learning process is facilitated in proportion to the amount of feedback that the learner is given about his performance.
Following are three statements concerning the learning process:
    I. The more specific the learner's knowledge of how he performed, the more rapid his improvement and the higher his level of performance
    II. Giving the learner knowledge of his results does not affect his motivation to learn.
    III. Learners who are not given feedback will set up subjective criteria and evaluate their own performance.
Which of the following choices lists ALL of the above statements that are generally CORRECT?
    A. I and II only   B. I and III only   C. II and III only   D. I, II, and III

KEY (CORRECT ANSWERS)

1.	D	11.	B	21.	C
2.	D	12.	B	22.	D
3.	C	13.	D	23.	C
4.	D	14.	C	24.	C
5.	D	15.	B	25.	C
6.	B	16.	A	26.	A
7.	A	17.	C	27.	A
8.	B	18.	C	28.	A
9.	A	19.	C	29.	A
10.	D	20.	C	30.	B

TEST 2

DIRECTIONS: Each question or incomplete statement is followed by several suggested answers or completions. Select the one that BEST answers the question or completes the statement. *PRINT THE LETTER OF THE CORRECT ANSWER IN THE SPACE AT THE RIGHT.*

Questions 1-6.

DIRECTIONS: Questions 1 through 6 are to be answered SOLELY on the basis of the information given in the following paragraph.

The use of role-playing as a training technique was developed during the past decade by social scientists, particularly psychologists, who have been active in training experiments. Originally, this technique was applied by clinical psychologists who discovered that a patient appears to gain understanding of an emotionally disturbing situation when encouraged to act out roles in that situation. As applied in government and business organizations, the purpose of role-playing is to aid employees to understand certain work problems involving interpersonal relations and to enable observers to evaluate various reactions to them. Thus, for example, on the problem of handling grievances, two individuals from the group might be selected to act out extemporaneously the parts of subordinate and supervisor. When this situation is enacted by various pairs among the class and the techniques and results are discussed, the members of the group are presumed to reach conclusions about the most effective means of handling similar situations. Often the use of role reversal, where participants take parts different from their actual work roles, assists individuals to gain more insight into other people's problems and viewpoints. Although role-playing can be a rewarding training device, the trainer must be aware of his responsibilities. If this technique is to be successful, thorough briefing of both actors and observers as to the situation in question, the participants' roles, and what to look for, is essential.

1. The role-playing technique was FIRST used for the purpose of
   A. measuring the effectiveness of training programs
   B. training supervisors in business organizations
   C. treating emotionally disturbed patients
   D. handling employee grievances

2. When role-playing is used in private business as a training device, the CHIEF aim is to
   A. develop better relations between supervisor and subordinate in the handling of grievances
   B. come up with a solution to a specific problem that has arisen
   C. determine the training needs of the group
   D. increase employee understanding of the human relation factors in work situations

3. From the above passage, it is MOST reasonable to conclude that when role-playing is used, it is preferable to have the roles acted out by
   A. only one set of actors   B. no more than 2 sets of actors
   C. several different sets of actors D. the trainer or trainers of the group

2 (#2)

4. Based on the above passage, a trainer using the technique of role reversal in a problem of first-line supervision should assign a senior employee to play the part of a(n)
   A. new employee
   B. senior employee
   C. principal employee
   D. angry citizen

   4.____

5. It can be inferred from the above passage that a limitation of role-play as a training method is that
   A. many work situations do not lend themselves to role-play
   B. employees are not experienced enough as actors to play the roles realistically
   C. only trainers who have psychological training can use it successfully
   D. participants who are observing and not acting do not benefit from it

   5.____

6. To obtain good results from the use of role-playing in training, a trainer should give participants
   A. a minimum of information about the situation so that they can act spontaneously
   B. scripts which illustrate the best method for handling the situation
   C. a complete explanation of the problem and the roles to be acted out
   D. a summary of work problems which involve interpersonal relations

   6.____

7. Of the following, the MOST important reason for a supervisor to prepare good written reports is that
   A. a supervisor is rated on the quality of his reports
   B. decisions are often made on the basis of the reports
   C. such reports take less time for superiors to review
   D. such reports demonstrate efficiency of department operations

   7.____

8. Of the following, the BEST test of a good report is whether it
   A. provides the information needed
   B. shows the good sense of the writer
   C. is prepared according to a proper format
   D. is grammatical and neat

   8.____

9. When a supervisor writes a report, he can BEST show that he has an understanding of the subject of the report by
   A. including necessary facts and omitting non-essential details
   B. using statistical data
   C. giving his conclusions but not the data on which they are based
   D. using a technical vocabulary

   9.____

10. Suppose you and another supervisor on the same level are assigned to work together on a report. You disagree strongly with one of the recommendations the other supervisor wants to include in the report but you cannot change his views.
    Of the following, it would be BEST that
    A. you refuse to accept responsibility for the report
    B. you ask that someone else be assigned to this project to replace you

    10.____

C. each of you state his own ideas about this recommendation in the report
D. you give in to the other supervisor's opinion for the sake of harmony

11. Standardized forms are often provided for submitting reports.
    Of the following, the MOST important advantage of using standardized forms for reports is that
    A. they take less time to prepare than individually written reports
    B. necessary information is less likely to be omitted
    C. the responsibility for preparing these reports can be delegated to subordinates
    D. the person making the report can omit information he considers unimportant

12. A report which may BEST be classed as a *periodic* report is one which
    A. requires the same type of information at regular intervals
    B. contains detailed information which is to be retained in permanent records
    C. is prepared whenever a special situation occurs
    D. lists information in graphic form

13. Which one of the following is NOT an important reason for keeping accurate records in an office?
    A. Facts will be on hand when decisions have to be made.
    B. The basis for past actions can be determined.
    C. Information needed by other bureaus can be furnished.
    D. Filing is easier when records are properly made out.

14. Suppose you are preparing to write a report recommending a change in a certain procedure. You learn that another supervisor made a report a few years ago suggesting a change in this same procedure, but that no action was taken.
    Of the following, it would be MOST desirable for you to
    A. avoid reading the other supervisor's report so that you will write with a more up-to-date point of view
    B. make no recommendation since management seems to be against any change in the procedure
    C. read the other report before you write your report to see what bearing it may have on your recommendations
    D. avoid including in your report any information that can be obtained by referring to the other report

15. If a report you are preparing to your superior is going to be a very long one, it would be DESIRABLE to include a summary of your basic conclusions
    A. at the end of the report
    B. at the beginning of the report
    C. in a separate memorandum
    D. right after you present the supporting data

16. Suppose that some bureau and department policies must be very frequently applied by your subordinates while others rarely come into use.
As a supervising employee, a GOOD technique for you to use in fulfilling your responsibility of seeing to it that policies are adhered to is to
    A. ask the director of the bureau to issue to all employees an explanation in writing of all policies
    B. review with your subordinates every week those policies which have daily application
    C. follow up on and explain at regular intervals the application of those policies which are not used very often by your subordinates
    D. recommend to your superiors that policies rarely used be changed or dropped

17. The BASIC purpose behind the principle of delegation of authority is to
    A. give the supervisor who is delegating a chance to acquire skills in higher level functions
    B. free the supervisor from routine tasks in order that he may do the important parts of his job
    C. prevent supervisors from overstepping the lines of authority which have been established
    D. place the work delegated in the hands of those employees who can perform it best

18. A district commander can BEST assist management in long-range planning by
    A. reporting to his superiors any changing conditions in the district
    B. maintaining a neat and efficiently run office
    C. scheduling work so that areas with a high rate of non-compliance get more intensive coverage
    D. properly training new personnel assigned to his district

19. Suppose that new quarters have been rented for your district office.
Of the following, the LEAST important factor to be considered in planning the layout of the office is the
    A. need for screening confidential activities from unauthorized persons
    B. relative importance of the various types of work
    C. areas of noise concentration
    D. convenience with which communication between sections of the office can be achieved

20. Of the following, the MOST basic effect of organizing a department so that lines of authority are clearly defined and duties are specifically assigned is to
    A. increase the need for close supervision
    B. decreases the initiative of subordinates
    C. lessen the possibility of duplication of work
    D. increase the responsibilities of supervisory personnel

21. An accepted management principle is that decisions should be delegated to the lowest point in the organization at which they can be made effectively.
The one of the following which is MOST likely to be a result of the application of this principle is that
    A. no factors will be overlooked in making decisions
    B. prompt action will follow the making of decisions
    C. decisions will be made more rapidly
    D. coordination of decisions that are made will be simplified

22. Suppose you are a supervisor and need some guidance from a higher authority. In which one of the following situations would it be PERMISSIBLE for you to bypass the regular upward channels of communication in the chain of command?
    A. In an emergency when your superior is not available
    B. When it is not essential to get a quick reply
    C. When you feel your immediate superior is not understanding of the situation
    D. When you want to obtain information that you think your superior does not have

23. Of the following, the CHIEF limitation of the organization chart as it is generally used in business and government is that the chart
    A. makes lines of responsibility and authority undesirably definite and formal
    B. is often out of date as soon as it is completed
    C. does not show human factors and informal working relationships
    D. is usually too complicated

24. The *span of control* for any supervisor is the
    A. number of tasks he is expected to perform himself
    B. amount of office space he and his subordinates occupy
    C. amount of work he is responsible for getting out
    D. number of subordinates he can supervise effectively

25. Of the following duties performed by a supervising employee, which would be considered a LINE function rather than a staff function?
    A. Evaluation of office personnel
    B. Recommendations for disciplinary action
    C. Initiating budget requests for replacement of equipment
    D. Inspections, at irregular times, of conditions and staff in the field

KEY (CORRECT ANSWERS)

1. C
2. D
3. C
4. A
5. A

6. C
7. B
8. A
9. A
10. C

11. B
12. A
13. D
14. C
15. B

16. C
17. B
18. A
19. B
20. C

21. B
22. A
23. C
24. D
25. D

EXAMINATION SECTION
TEST 1

DIRECTIONS: Each question or incomplete statement is followed by several suggested answers or completions. Select the one that BEST answers the question or completes the statement. *PRINT THE LETTER OF THE CORRECT ANSWER IN THE SPACE AT THE RIGHT.*

1. As a supervisor in a bureau, you have been asked by the head of the bureau to recommend whether or not the work of the bureau requires an increase in the permanent staff of the bureau.
   Of the following questions, the one whose answer would MOST likely assist you in making your recommendation is: Are
   A. some permanent employees working irregular hours because they occasionally work overtime?
   B. the present permanent employees satisfied with their work assignment?
   C. temporary employees hired to handle seasonal fluctuations in work load?
   D. the present permanent employees keeping the work of the bureau current?

   1.____

2. In making job assignments to his subordinates, a supervisor should follow the principle that each individual GENERALLY is capable of
   A. performing one type of work well and less capable of performing other types well
   B. learning to perform a wide variety of different types of work
   C. performing best the type of work in which he has had experience
   D. learning to perform any type of work in which he is given training

   2.____

3. Assume that you are the supervisor of a large number of clerks in a unit in a city agency. Your unit has just been given an important assignment which must be completed a week from now. You know that, henceforth, your unit will be given this assignment every six months.
   You or any one of your subordinates who has been properly instructed can complete this assignment in one day. This assignment is of a routine type which is ordinarily handled by clerks. There is enough time for you to train one of your subordinates to handle the assignment and then have him do it. However, it would take twice as much time for you to take this course of action as it would for you to do the assignment yourself.
   The one of the following courses of action which you should take in this situation is to
   A. do the assignment yourself as soon as possible without discussing it with any of your subordinates at this time
   B. do the assignment yourself and then train one of your subordinates to handle it in the future
   C. give the assignment to one of your subordinates after training him to handle it
   D. train each of your subordinates to do the assignment on a rotating basis after you have done it yourself the first time

   3.____

4. You are in charge of an office in which each member of the staff has a different set of duties, although each has the same title. No member of the staff can perform the duties of any other member of the staff without first receiving extensive training. Assume that it is necessary for one member of the staff to take on, in addition to his regular work, an assignment which any member of the staff is capable of carrying out.
The one of the following considerations which would have the MOST weight in determining which staff member is to be given the additional assignment is the
   A. quality of the work performed by the individual members of the staff
   B. time consumed by individual members of the staff in performing their work
   C. level of difficulty of the duties being performed by individual members of the staff
   D. relative importance of the duties being performed by individual members of the staff

4.____

5. The one of the following causes of clerical error which is usually considered to be LEAST attributable to faulty supervision or inefficient management is
   A. inability to carry out instructions
   B. too much work to do
   C. an inappropriate recordkeeping system
   D. continual interruptions

5.____

6. Suppose you are in charge of a large unit in which all of the clerical staff perform similar tasks.
In evaluating the relative accuracy of the clerks, the clerk who should be considered to be the LEAST accurate is the one
   A. whose errors result in the greatest financial loss
   B. whose errors cost the most to locate
   C. who makes the greatest percentage of errors in his work
   D. who makes the greatest number of errors in the unit

6.____

7. Assume that under a proposed procedure for handling employee grievances in a public agency, the first step to be taken is for the aggrieved employee to submit his grievance as soon as it arises to a grievance board set up to hear all employee grievances in the agency. The board, which is to consist of representatives of management and of rank and file employees, is to consider the grievance, obtain all necessary pertinent information, and then render a decision on the matter. Thus, the first-line supervisor would not be involved in the settlement of any of his subordinates' grievances except when asked by the board to submit information.
This proposed procedure would be generally UNDESIRABLE chiefly because the
   A. board may become a bottleneck to delay the prompt disposition of grievances
   B. aggrieved employees and their supervisors have not been first given the opportunity to resolve the grievances themselves

7.____

C. employees would be likely to submit imaginary, as well as real, grievances to the board
D. board will lack first-hand, personal knowledge of the factors involved in grievances

8. Sometimes jobs in private organizations and public agencies are broken down so as to permit a high degree of job specialization.
   Of the following, an IMPORTANT effect of a high degree of job specialization in a public agency is that employees performing
   A. highly specialized jobs may not be readily transferable to other jobs in the agency
   B. similar duties may require closer supervision than employees performing unrelated functions
   C. specialized duties can be held responsible for their work to a greater extent than can employees performing a wide variety of functions
   D. specialized duties will tend to cooperate readily with employees performing other types of specialized duties

9. Assume that you are the supervisor of a clerical unit in an agency. One of your subordinates violates a rule of the agency, a violation which requires that the employee be suspended from his work for one day. The violated rule is one that you have found to be unduly strict, and you have recommended to the management of agency that the rule be changed or abolished. The management has been considering your recommendation but has not yet reached a decision on the matter.
   In these circumstances, you should
   A. not initiate disciplinary action but, instead, explain to the employee that the rule may be changed shortly
   B. delay disciplinary action on the violation until the management has reached a decision on changing the rule
   C. modify the disciplinary action by reprimanding the employee and informing him that further action may be taken when the management has reached a decision on changing the rule
   D. initiate the prescribed disciplinary action with commenting on the strictness of the rule or on your recommendation

10. Assume that a supervisor praises his subordinates for satisfactory aspects of their work only when he is about to criticize them for unsatisfactory aspects of their work.
    Such a practice is UNDESIRABLE primarily because
    A. his subordinates may expect to be praised for their work even if it is unsatisfactory
    B. praising his subordinates for some aspects of their work while criticizing other aspects will weaken the effects of the criticisms
    C. his subordinates would be more receptive to criticism if it were followed by praise
    D. his subordinates may come to disregard praise and wait for criticism to be given

4 (#1)

11. The one of the following which would be the BEST reason for an agency to eliminate a procedure for obtaining and recording certain information is that
    A. it is no longer legally required to obtain the information
    B. there is no advantage in obtaining the information
    C. the information could be compiled on the basis of other information available
    D. the information obtained is sometimes incorrect

11.____

12. In determining the type and number of records to be kept in an agency, it is important to recognize that records are of value PRIMARILY as
    A. raw material to be used in statistical analysis
    B. sources of information about the agency's activities
    C. by-products of the activities carried on by the agency
    D. data for evaluating the effectiveness of the agency

12.____

13. Aside from requirements imposed by authority, the frequency with which reports are submitted or the length of the interval which they cover should depend PRINCIPALLY on the
    A. availability of the data to be included in the reports
    B. amount of time required to prepare the reports
    C. extent of the variations in the data with the passage of time
    D. degree of comprehensiveness required in the reports

13.____

14. Organizations that occupy large, general, open-area offices sometimes consider it desirable to build private offices for the supervisors of large bureaus. The one of the following which is generally NOT considered to be a justification of the use of private office is that they
    A. lend prestige to the person occupying the office
    B. provide facilities for private conferences
    C. achieve the maximum use of office space
    D. provide facilities for performing work requiring a high degree of concentration

14.____

15. The LEAST important factor to be considered in planning the layout of an office is the
    A. relative importance of the different types of work to be done
    B. convenience with which communication can be achieved
    C. functional relationships of the activities of the office
    D. necessity for screening confidential activities from unauthorized persons

15.____

16. The one of the following which is generally considered to be the CHIEF advantage of using data processing equipment in modern offices is to
    A. facilitate the use of a wide variety of sources of information
    B. supply management with current information quickly
    C. provide uniformity in the processing and reporting of information
    D. broaden the area in which management decisions can be made

16.____

17. In the box design of office forms, the spaces in which information is to be entered are arranged in boxes containing captions.
Of the following, the one which is generally NOT considered to be an acceptable rule in employing box design is that
   A. space should be allowed for the lengthiest anticipated entry in a box
   B. the caption should be located in the upper left corner of the box
   C. the boxes on a form should be of the same size and shape
   D. boxes should be aligned vertically whenever possible

17.____

18. As a management tool, the work count would generally be of LEAST assistance to a unit supervisor in
   A. scheduling the work of his unit
   B. locating bottlenecks in the work of his unit
   C. ascertaining the number of subordinates he needs
   D. tracing the flow of work in the unit

18.____

19. Of the following, the FIRST step that should be taken in a forms simplification program is to make a
   A. detailed analysis of the items found on current forms
   B. study of the amount of use made of existing forms
   C. survey of the amount of each kid of form on hand
   D. survey of the characteristics of the more effective forms in use

19.____

20. The work-distribution chart is a valuable tool for an office supervisor to use in conducting work simplification programs.
Of the following questions, the one which a work-distribution chart would generally be LEAST useful in answering is:
   A. What activities take the most time?
   B. Are the employees doing many unrelated tasks?
   C. Is work being distributed evenly among the employees?
   D. Are activities being performed in proper sequence?

20.____

21. Assume that, as a supervisor, you conduct, from time to time, work-performance studies in various sections of your agency. The units of measurement used in any study depend on the particular study and may be number of letters typed, number of papers filed, or other suitable units.
It is MOST important that the units of measurement to be used in a study conform to the units used in similar past studies when the
   A. units of measurement to be used in the study cannot be defined sharply
   B. units of measurement used in past studies were satisfactory
   C results of the study are to be compared with those of past studies
   D. results of the study are to be used for the same purpose as were those of past studies

21.____

22. As it is used in auditing, an internal check is a
   A. procedure which is designed to guard against fraud
   B. periodic audit by a public accounting firm to verify the accuracy of the internal transactions of an organization

22.____

C. document transferring funds from one section to another within an organization
D. practice of checking documents twice before they are transmitted outside an organization

23. Of the following, the one which can LEAST be considered to be a proper function of an accounting system is to
    A. indicate the need to curtail expenditures
    B. provide information for future fiscal programs
    C. record the expenditure of funds from special appropriations
    D. suggest method to expedite the collection of revenues

24. Assume that a new unit is to be established in an agency. The unit is to compile and tabulate data so that it will be of the greatest usefulness to the high-level administrators in the agency in making administrative decisions. In planning the organization of this unit, the question that should be answered FIRST is:
    A. What interpretations are likely to be made of the data by the high-level administrators in making decisions?
    B. At what point in the decision-making process will it be most useful to inject the data?
    C. What types of data will be required by high-level administrators in making decisions?
    D. What criteria will the high-level administrators use to evaluate the decisions they make?

25. The one of the following which is the CHIEF limitation of the organization chart as it is generally used in business and government is that the chart
    A. engenders within incumbents feelings of rights to positions they occupy
    B. reveals only formal authority relationships, omitting the informal ones
    C. shows varying degrees of authority even though authority is not subject to such differentiation
    D. presents organizational structure as it is rather than what it is supposed to be

26. The degree of decentralization that is effective and economical in an organization tends to vary INVERSELY with the
    A. size of the organization
    B. availability of adequate numbers of competent personnel
    C. physical dispersion of the organization's activities
    D. adequacy of the organization's communications system

27. The one of the following which usually can LEAST be considered to be an advantage of committees as they are generally used in government and business is that they
    A. provide opportunities for reconciling varying points of view
    B. promote coordination by the interchange of information among the members of the committee

C. act promptly in situations requiring immediate action
D. use group judgment to resolve questions requiring a wide range of experience

28. Managerial decentralization is defined as the decentralization of decision-making authority.
    The degree of managerial decentralization in an organization varies INVERSELY with the
    A. number of decisions made lower down the managerial hierarchy
    B. importance of the decisions made lower down the management hierarchy
    C. number of major organizational functions affected by decisions made at lower management levels
    D. amount of review to which decisions made at lower management levels are subjected

28.____

29. Some policy-making commissions are composed of members who are appointed to overlapping terms.
    Of the following, the CHIEF advantage of appointing members to overlapping terms in such commissions is that
    A. continuity of policy is promoted
    B. the likelihood of compromise policy decisions is reduced
    C. responsibility for policy decisions can be fixed upon individual members
    D. the likelihood of unanimity of opinion is increased

29.____

30. If a certain public agency with a fixed number of employees has a line organizational structure, then the width of the span of supervision is
    A. *inversely* proportional to the length of the chain of command in the organization
    B. *directly* proportional to the complexity of tasks performed in the organization
    C. *inversely* proportional to the competence of the personnel in the organization
    D. *directly* proportional to the number of levels of supervision existing in the organization

30.____

31. Mr. Brown is a supervisor in charge of a section of clerical employees in an agency. The section consists of four units, each headed by a unit supervisor. From time to time, he makes tours of his section for the purpose of maintaining contact with the rank and file employees. During these tours, he discusses with these employees their work production, work methods, work problems, and other related topics. The information he obtains in this manner is often incomplete or inaccurate. At meeting with the unit supervisors, he questions them on the information acquired during his tours. The supervisors are often unable to answer the questions immediately because they are based on incomplete or inaccurate information. When the supervisors ask that they be permitted to accompany Mr. Brown on his tours and thus answer his questions on the spot, Mr. Brown refuses, explaining that a rank and file employee might be reluctant to speak freely in the presence of his supervisor.

31.____

This situation may BEST be described as a violation of the principle of organization called
A. span of control
B. delegation of authority
C. specialization of work
D. unity of command

Questions 32-36.

DIRECTIONS: Each of Questions 32 through 36 consists of a statement which contains one word that is incorrectly used because it is not in keeping with the meaning that the quotation is evidently intended to convey. For each of these questions, you are to select the INCORRECTLY used word and substitute for it one of the word lettered A, B, C, or D, which helps BEST to convey the meaning of the statement.

32. There has developed in recent years an increasing awareness of the need to measure the quality of management in all enterprise and to seek the principles that can serve as a basis for this improvement.
A. growth   B. raise   C. efficiency   D. define

33. It is hardly an exaggeration to deny that the permanence, productivity, and humanity of any industrial system depend upon its ability to utilize the positive and constructive impulses of all who work and upon its ability to arouse and continue interest in the necessary activities.
A. develop   B. efficiency   C. state   D. inspirational

34. The selection of managers on the basis of technical knowledge alone seems to recognize that the essential characteristic of management is getting things done through others, thereby demanding skills that are essential in coordinating the activities of subordinates.
A. training
B. fails
C. organization
D. improving

35. Only when it is deliberate and when it is clearly understood what impressions the ease of communication will probably create in the minds of employees and subordinate management, should top management refrain from commenting on a subject that is of general concern.
A. obvious   B. benefit   C. doubt   D. absence

36. Scientific planning of work requires careful analysis of facts and a precise plan of action for the whims and fancies of executives that often provide only a vague indication of the work to be done.
A. substitutes
B. development
C. preliminary
D. comprehensive

37. Within any single level of government, as a city or a state, the administrative authority may be concentrated or dispersed.
Of the following plans of government, the one in which administrative authority would be dispersed the MOST is the ____ plan.
   A. mayor
   B. mayor-council
   C. commission
   D. city manager

37.____

38. In general, the courts may review a decision of an administrative agency with rule-making powers. However, the courts will usually refuse to review a decision of such an agency if the only question raised concerning the decision is whether or not the
   A. decision contravenes public policy
   B. agency has abused the powers conferred upon it
   C. decision deals with an issue which is within the jurisdiction of the agency
   D. agency has applied the same rules of evidence as are used in the courts

38.____

39. A legislature sometimes delegates rule-making powers to the administrators of a public agency.
Of the following, the CHIEF advantage of such delegation is that
   A. the frequency with which the legality of the agency's rules is contested in court will be reduced
   B. the agency will have the flexibility to adjust to changing conditions and problems
   C. mistakes made by the administrators or the legislature in defining the scope of the agency's program may be easily corrected
   D. the legislature will not be required to approve the rules formulated by the agency

39.____

40. Some municipalities have delegated the functions of budget preparation and personnel selection to central agencies, thus removing these functions from operating departments.
Of the following, the MOST important reason by municipalities have delegated these functions to central agencies is that
   A. the performance of these functions presents problems that vary from one operating department to another
   B. operating departments often lack sufficient funds to perform these functions adequately
   C. the performance of these functions by a central agency produces more uniform policies than if these functions are performed by the operating departments
   D. central agencies are not controlled as closely as are operating departments and so have greater freedom in formulating new policies and procedures to deal with difficult budget and personnel problems

40.____

41. Of the following, the MOST fundamental reason for the use of budgets in governmental administration is that budgets
    A. minimize seasonal variations in workloads and expenditures of public agencies
    B. facilitate decentralization of functions performed by public agencies
    C. provide advance control on the expenditure of funds
    D. establish valid bases for comparing present governmental activities with corresponding activities in previous periods

42. In some governmental jurisdictions, the chief executive prepares the budget for a fiscal period and presents it to the legislative branch of government for adoption. In other jurisdictions, the legislative branch prepares and adopts the budget.
    Preparation of the budget by the chief executive rather than by the legislative branch is
    A. *desirable*, primarily because the chief executive is held largely accountable by the public for the results of fiscal operations and should, therefore, be the one to prepare the budget
    B. *undesirable*, primarily because such a separation of the legislative and executive branches leads to the enactment of a budget that does not consider the overall needs of the government
    C. *desirable*, primarily because the preparation of the budget by the chief executive limits legislative review and evaluation of operating programs
    D. *undesirable*, primarily because responsibility for budget preparation should be placed in the branch that must eventually adopt the budget and appropriate the funds for it

43. The one of the following which is generally the FIRST step in the budget-making process of a municipality that has a central budget agency is
    A. determination of available sources of revenue within the municipality
    B. establishment of tax rates at levels sufficient to achieve a balanced budget in the following fiscal period
    C. evaluation by the central budget agency of the adequacy of the municipality's previous budgets
    D. assembling by the central budget agency of the proposed expenditures of each agency in the municipality for the following fiscal period

44. It is advantageous for a municipality to issue serial bonds rather than sinking fund bonds CHIEFLY because
    A. an issue of serial bonds usually includes a wider range of maturity dates than does an issue of sinking fund bond
    B. appropriations set aside periodically to retire serial bonds as they fall due are more readily invested in long-term securities at favorable rates of interest than are appropriations earmarked for redemption of sinking fund bonds
    C. serial bond are sold at regular intervals while sinking fund bonds are issued as the need for fund arises
    D. a greater variety of interest rates is usually offered in an issue of serial bonds than in an issue of sinking fund bond

45. Studies conducted by the Regional Plan Association of the 22-county New York Metropolitan Region, comprising New York City and surrounding counties in New York, New Jersey, and Connecticut, have defined Manhattan, Brooklyn, Queens, the Bronx, and Hudson County in New Jersey as the core. Such studies have examined the per capita personal income of the core as a percent of the per capita personal income of the entire Region, and the population of the core as a percent of the total population of the entire Region.
    These studies support the conclusion that, as a percent of the entire Region,
    A. both population and per capita personal income in the core were higher in 2020 than in 1990
    B. both population and per capita personal income in the core were lower in 2020 than in 1990
    C. population was higher and per capita personal income was lower in the core in 2020 than in 1990
    D. population was lower and per capita personal income was higher in the core in 2020 than in 1990

45.____

KEY (CORRECT ANSWERS)

1.	D	11.	B	21.	C	31.	D	41.	C
2.	B	12.	B	22.	A	32.	B	42.	A
3.	C	13.	C	23.	D	33.	C	43.	D
4.	B	14.	C	24.	C	34.	B	44.	A
5.	A	15.	A	25.	B	35.	D	45.	B
6.	C	16.	B	26.	D	36.	A		
7.	B	17.	C	27.	C	37.	C		
8.	A	18.	D	28.	D	38.	D		
9.	D	19.	B	29.	A	39.	B		
10.	D	20.	D	30.	A	40.	C		

EXAMINATION SECTION
TEST 1

DIRECTIONS: Each question or incomplete statement is followed by several suggested answers or completions. Select the one that BEST answers the question or completes the statement. *PRINT THE LETTER OF THE CORRECT ANSWER IN THE SPACE AT THE RIGHT.*

1. The CHIEF assumption underlying the provisions for a salary range with a minimum, a maximum, and intervening steps for each class in the compensation plans of MOST public agencies is that

    A. the granting of periodic increments to employees encourages staff stability at the lowest possible cost
    B. job offers made at a step higher than the minimum of a salary range are a positive aid to recruitment
    C. automatic salary increments provide an incentive to employees to improve their job performances from year to year
    D. an employee's value to his employer tends to increase with the passage of time

2. Selection of candidates for employment on the basis of aptitude test results is made on the assumption that the candidates making the highest test scores

    A. possess the most knowledge about the job for which they were tested
    B. will need a minimum amount of training on the job for which they were tested
    C. will be the most satisfactory employees after they have received training
    D. are those who will have the highest interest in succeeding on the job for which they were tested

3. In position classification, the one of the following factors which is of LEAST importance in classifying a clerical position is the

    A. degree of supervision under which the work of the position is performed
    B. amount of supervision exercised over other positions
    C. training and experience of the incumbent of the position
    D. extent to which independent judgment must be exercised in performing the duties of the position

4. The position classifying bureau of the central personnel agency in a public jurisdiction is normally NOT responsible for

    A. allocating individual positions to classes
    B. assigning titles to classes of positions
    C. establishing minimum qualifications for positions
    D. determining which positions are necessary

5. The one of the following which is generally considered to be an ESSENTIAL element in the process of classifying a position in a civil service system is the

    A. comparison of the position with similar and related positions
    B. evaluation of the skill with which the duties of the position are being performed
    C. number of positions similar to the position being classified
    D. determination of the salary being paid for the position

2 (#1)

6. Of the following, the LEAST important objective of a modern service rating system which is applied to civil service positions is to

   A. validate selection procedures
   B. improve the quality of supervision
   C. furnish a basis for the construction of a position classification plan
   D. foster the development of good employee performance

7. Some public agencies conduct exit interviews with employees who quit their jobs. The one of the following which is generally considered to be the CHIEF value to a public agency of such an interview is in

   A. ascertaining from the employee the reasons why he is leaving his job
   B. obtaining reliable information on the employee's work history with the agency
   C. persuading the employee to reconsider his decision to quit
   D. giving the employee a final evaluation of his work performance

8. The rate of labor turnover in an organization may be arrived at by dividing the total number of separations from the organization in a given period by the average number of workers employed in the same period. In arriving at the rate, it is assumed that those separated are replaced.
If the rate of turnover is excessively low in comparison with other similar organizations, it USUALLY indicates that

   A. the organization is stagnant
   B. promotions within the organization are made frequently
   C. the organization's recruitment policies have been ineffective
   D. suitable workers are in short supply

9. Of the following aspects of a training program for supervisory personnel in a public agency, the aspect for which it is usually the MOST difficult to develop adequate information is the

   A. determination of the training needs of the supervisory personnel in the agency
   B. establishment of the objectives of the program
   C. selection of suitable training methods for the program
   D. evaluation of the effectiveness of the training program

10. You are conducting a training conference for new supervisors on supervisory techniques and problems. When one of the participants in the conference proposes what you consider to be an unsatisfactory solution for the problem under discussion, none of the other participants questions the solution or offers an alternate solution.
For you to tell the group why the solution is unsatisfactory would be

   A. *desirable* chiefly because satisfactory rather than unsatisfactory solutions to the problems should be stressed in the conference
   B. *undesirable* chiefly because the participants them-selves should be stimulated to present reasons why the proposed solution is unsatisfactory
   C. *desirable* chiefly because you, as the conference leader, should guide the participants in solving conference problems
   D. *undesirable* chiefly because the proposed unsatisfactory solution may be useful in illustrating the advantages of a satisfactory solution

11. It is generally BEST that the greater part of in-service training for the operating employees of an agency in a public jurisdiction be given by   11.____

    A. a team of trainers from the central personnel agency of the jurisdiction
    B. training specialists on the staff of the personnel unit of the agency
    C. a team of teachers from the public school system of the jurisdiction
    D. members of the regular supervisory force of the agency

12. You are responsible for training a number of your subordinates to handle some complicated procedures which your unit will adopt after the training has been completed. If approximately 30 hours of training are required and you can arrange the training sessions during working hours as you see fit, learning would ordinarily be BEST effected if you scheduled the trainees to devote _____ to the training until it is completed.   12.____

    A. a half day each week   B. one full day each week
    C. a half day every day   D. full time

13. Assume that you are giving a lecture for the purpose of explaining a new procedure. You find that the employees attending the lecture are asking many questions on the material as you present it. Consequently, you realize that you will be unable to cover all of the material you had intended to cover, and that a second lecture will be necessary.
    In this situation, the MOST advisable course of action for you to take would be to   13.____

    A. answer the questions on the new procedure as they arise
    B. answer the questions that can be answered quickly and ask the employees to reserve questions requiring lengthier answers for the second lecture
    C. suggest that further questions be withheld until the second lecture so that you can cover as much of the remaining material as possible
    D. refer the questions back to the employees asking them

14. As a supervisor, you are conducting a training conference dealing with administrative principles and practices.
    One of the members of the conference, Mr. Smith, makes a factual statement which you know to be incorrect and which may hinder the development of the discussion. None of the other members attempts to correct Mr. Smith or to question him on what he has said, although until this point, the members have participated actively in the discussions. In this situation, the MOST advisable course of action for you to take would be to   14.____

    A. proceed with the discussion without commenting on Mr. Smith's statement
    B. correct the statement that Mr. Smith has made
    C. emphasize that the material discussed at the conference is to serve only as a guide for handling actual work situations
    D. urge the members to decide for themselves whether or not to accept factual statements made at the conference

15. With the wholehearted support of top management, the training bureau of a public agency schedules a series of training conferences for all the supervisory and administrative employees in order to alter their approaches to the problems arising from the interaction of supervisors and subordinates. During the conferences, the participants discuss solutions to typical problems of this type and become conscious of the principles underlying these solutions. After the series of conferences is concluded, it is found that the first-line supervisors are not applying the principles to the problems they are encountering on the job.
Of the following, the MOST likely reason why these supervisors are not putting the principles into practice is that

    A. the training conferences have not changed the attitudes of these supervisors
    B. these supervisors are reluctant to put into practice methods with which their subordinates are unfamiliar
    C. the conference method is not suitable for human relations training
    D. the principles which were covered in the conferences are not suitable for solving actual work problems

15._____

16. Assume that you are the leader of a training conference dealing with supervisory techniques and problems. One of the problems being discussed is one with which you have had no experience, but two of the participants have had considerable experience with it. These two participants carry on an extended discussion of the problem in light of their experiences, and it is obvious from their discussion that they understand the problem thoroughly. It is also obvious that the other participants in the conference are very much interested in the discussion and are taking notes on the material presented.
For you to permit the two participants to continue until the amount of time allowed for discussion of the problem has been exhausted would be

    A. *desirable* chiefly because their discussion, which is based on actual work experience, may be more meaningful to the other participants than would a discussion which is not based on work experience
    B. *undesirable* chiefly because they are discussing the material only in the light of their own experiences rather than in general terms
    C. *desirable* chiefly because the introduction of the material by two of the participants themselves may put the other participants at ease
    D. *undesirable* chiefly because the other participants are not joining in the discussion of the problem

16._____

17. You are a supervisor in charge of a unit of clerical employees. One of your subordinates, Mr. Smith, has not seemed to be his usual self in the past several weeks, but rather has seemed to be disturbed. In addition, he has not been producing his usual quantity of work and has been provoking arguments with his colleagues. He approaches you and asks if he may discuss with you a problem which he believes has been affecting his work. As Mr. Smith begins to discuss the problem, you immediately realize that, although it may be disturbing to him, it is really a trivial matter.
Of the following, the FIRST step that you should take in this situation is to

    A. permit Mr. Smith to continue to describe his problem, interrupting him only when clarification of a point is needed
    B. tell Mr. Smith that his becoming unduly upset about the problem will not help to solve it

17._____

C. point out that you and your subordinates have faced more serious problems and that this one is a relatively minor matter
D. suggest that the problem should be solved before it develops into a serious matter

18. A line supervisor can play an important role in helping his subordinates to make healthy mental, emotional, and social adjustments.
The one of the following which would NOT be considered to be a part of the supervisor's role in helping his subordinates to make these adjustments is to

   A. ascertain which subordinates are likely to develop maladjustments
   B. recognize indications of these types of maladjustments
   C. refer subordinates displaying signs of maladjustments that he cannot handle to specialists for assistance
   D. create a work environment that will tend to minimize his subordinates' preoccupations with personal problems

19. One of the principal duties of the management in a public agency is to secure the most effective utilization of personnel.
The one of the following which would contribute LEAST to effective utilization and development of personnel in a public agency is

   A. the use of training programs designed to prepare employees for future tasks
   B. a comprehensive list of skills and abilities needed to perform the work of the agency effectively
   C. a systematic effort to discover employees of high potential and to develop them for future responsibilities
   D. the assignment of employees to duties which require the maximum use of their abilities

20. During a training session for new employees, an employee becomes upset because he is unable to solve a problem presented to him by the instructor.
Of the following actions which the instructor could take, the one which would be MOST likely to dispel the employee's emotional state is to

   A. give him a different type of problem which he may be able to solve
   B. minimize the importance of finding a solution to the problem and proceed to the next topic
   C. encourage the other participants to contribute to the solution
   D. provide him with hints which would enable him to solve the problem

21. Studies in human behavior have shown that an employee in a work group who is capable of producing substantially more work than is being produced by the average of the group GENERALLY will

   A. tend to produce substantially more work than is produced by the average member of the group
   B. attempt to become the informal leader of the group
   C. tend to produce less work than he is capable of producing
   D. attempt to influence the other members of the group to increase their production

22. Studies of organizations show that formal employee participation in the formulation of work policies before they are put into effect is MOST likely to result in a(n)

    A. reduction in the length of time required to formulate the policies
    B. increase in the number of employees affected by the policies
    C. reduction in the length of time required to implement the policies
    D. increase in the number of policies formulated within the organization

23. No matter how elaborate a formal system of communication is in an organization, the system will always be supplemented by informal channels of communication, such as the *grapevine*. Although such informal channels of communication are usually not highly regarded, they sometimes are of value to an organization.
Of the following, the CHIEF value of informal channels of communication is that they serve to

    A. transmit information that management has neglected to send through the formal system of communication
    B. confirm information that has already been received through the formal system of communication
    C. hinder the formation of employee cliques in the organization
    D. revise information sent through the formal system of communication

24. The one of the following which is generally considered to be the MOST important advantage of the written questionnaire method of obtaining information is that this method

    A. assures accuracy of response greater than that obtained from other methods
    B. gives the persons to whom the questionnaire is sent the opportunity to express their opinions and feelings
    C. makes it possible to obtain the responses of many persons at small cost
    D. permits errors in the information obtained to be corrected easily when they are discovered

25. In collecting objective data for the evaluation of procedures which are used in his agency, an administrator should, in every case, be careful

    A. to take an equal number of measurements from each source of information
    B. not to allow his beliefs about the values of the procedures to influence the choice of data
    C. to apply statistical methods continuously to the data as they are gathered to assure maximum accuracy
    D. not to accept data which are inconsistent with the general trend established by verified data

KEY CORRECT ANSWERS

1. D
2. C
3. C
4. D
5. A

6. C
7. A
8. A
9. D
10. B

11. D
12. C
13. A
14. B
15. A

16. D
17. A
18. A
19. B
20. D

21. C
22. C
23. A
24. C
25. B

TEST 2

DIRECTIONS: Each question or incomplete statement is followed by several suggested answers or completions. Select the one that BEST answers the question or completes the statement. *PRINT THE LETTER OF THE CORRECT ANSWER IN THE SPACE AT THE RIGHT*

1. Assume that the law enforcement division in a public jurisdiction employs only males who are 5 feet 8 inches or taller.
   To expect the heights of these employees to be normally distributed is UNJUSTIFIED primarily because

   A. the distribution of a random sample is not usually the same as the distribution of the population from which the sample was drawn
   B. no maximum height requirement has been established
   C. height is a characteristic which is not normally distributed in the general population of males
   D. the employees are not a representative sample of the general population of males

1.____

Questions 2-5.

DIRECTIONS: Questions 2 through 5 are to be answered SOLELY on the basis of the information contained in the following paragraph.

A standard comprises characteristics attached to an aspect of a process or product by which it can be evaluated. Standardization is the development and adoption of standards. When they are formulated, standards are not usually the product of a single person, but represent the thoughts and ideas of a group, leavened with the knowledge and information which are currently available. Standards which do not meet certain basic requirements become a hindrance rather than an aid to progress. Standards must not only be correct, accurate, and precise in requiring no more and no less than what is needed for satisfactory results, but they must also be workable in the sense that their usefulness is not nullified by external conditions. Standards should also be acceptable to the people who use them. If they are not acceptable, they cannot be considered to be satisfactory, although they may possess all the other essential characteristics.

2. According to the above paragraph, a processing standard that requires the use of materials that cannot be procured is MOST likely to be

   A. incomplete   B. inaccurate
   C. unworkable   D. unacceptable

2.____

3. According to the above paragraph, the construction of standards to which the performance of job duties should conform is MOST often

   A. the work of the people responsible for seeing that the duties are properly performed
   B. accomplished by the person who is best informed about the functions involved
   C. the responsibility of the people who are to apply them
   D. attributable to the efforts of various informed persons

3.____

4. According to the above paragraph, when standards call for finer tolerances than those essential to the conduct of successful production operations, the effect of the standards on the improvement of production operations is

   A. negative
   B. nullified
   C. negligible
   D. beneficial

5. The one of the following which is the MOST suitable title for the above paragraph is

   A. The Evaluation of Formulated Standards
   B. The Attributes of Satisfactory Standards
   C. The Adoption of Acceptable Standards
   D. The Use of Process or Product Standards

Questions 6-9.

DIRECTIONS: Questions 6 through 9 are to be answered SOLELY on the basis of the information contained in the following paragraph.

Good personnel relations of an organization depend upon mutual confidence, trust, and good will. The basis of confidence is understanding. Most troubles start with people who do not understand each other. When the organization's intentions or motives are misunderstood, or when reasons for actions, practices, or policies are misconstrued, complete cooperation from individuals is not forthcoming. If management expects full cooperation from employees, it has a responsibility of sharing with them the information which is the foundation of proper understanding, confidence, and trust. Personnel management has long since outgrown the days when it was the vogue to treat them rough and tell them nothing. Up-to-date personnel management provides all possible information about the activities, aims, and purposes of the organization. It seems altogether creditable that a desire should exist among employees for such information which the best-intentioned executive might think, would not interest them and which the worst-intentioned would think was none of their business.

6. The above paragraph implies that one of the causes of the difficulty which an organization might have with its personnel relations is that its employees

   A. have not expressed interest in the activities, aims, and purposes of the organization
   B. do not believe in the good faith of the organization
   C. have not been able to give full cooperation to the organization
   D. do not recommend improvements in the practices and policies of the organization

7. According to the above paragraph, in order for an organization to have good personnel relations, it is NOT essential that

   A. employees have confidence in the organization
   B. the purposes of the organization be understood by the employees
   C. employees have a desire for information about the organization
   D. information about the organization be communicated to employees

8. According to the paragraph, an organization which provides full information about itself to its employees

    A. understands the intentions of its employees
    B. satisfies a praiseworthy desire among its employees
    C. is managed by executives who have the best intentions toward its employees
    D. is confident that its employees understand its motives

9. The one of the following which is the MOST suitable title for the paragraph is

    A. The Foundations of Personnel Relations
    B. The Consequences of Employee Misunderstanding
    C. The Development of Personnel Management Practices
    D. The Acceptance of Organizational Objectives

Questions 10-13.

DIRECTIONS: Questions 10 through 13 are to be answered SOLELY on the basis of the information contained in the following paragraph.

Management, which is the function of executive leadership, has as its principal phases the planning, organizing, and controlling of the activities of subordinate groups in the accomplishment of organizational objectives. Planning specifies the kind and extent of the factors, forces, and effects, and the relationships among them, that will be required for satisfactory accomplishment. The nature of the objectives and their requirements must be known before determinations can be made as to what must be done, how it must be done and why, where actions should take place, who should be responsible, and similar problems pertaining to the formulation of a plan. Organizing, which creates the conditions that must be present before the execution of the plan can be undertaken successfully, cannot be done intelligently without knowledge of the organizational objectives. Control, which has to do with the constraint and regulation of activities entering into the execution of the plan, must be exercised in accordance with the characteristics and requirements of the activities demanded by the plan.

10. The one of the following which is the MOST suitable title for the paragraph is

    A. The Nature of Successful Organization
    B. The Planning of Management Functions
    C. The Importance of Organizational Objectives
    D. The Principle Aspects of Management

11. It can be inferred from the paragraph that the one of the following functions whose existence is essential to the existence of the other three is the

    A. regulation of the work needed to carry out a plan
    B. understanding of what the organization intends to accomplish
    C. securing of information of the factors necessary for accomplishment of objectives
    D. establishment of the conditions required for successful action

4 (#2)

12. The one of the following which would NOT be included within any of the principal phases of the function of executive leadership as defined in the paragraph is   12._____

    A. determination of manpower requirements
    B. procurement of required material
    C. establishment of organizational objectives
    D. scheduling of production

13. The conclusion which can MOST reasonably be drawn from the paragraph is that the control phase of managing is most directly concerned with the   13._____

    A. influencing of policy determinations
    B. administering of suggestion systems
    C. acquisition of staff for the organization
    D. implementation of performance standards

14. A study reveals that Miss Brown files N cards in M hours, and Miss Smith files the same number of cards in T hours. If the two employees work together, the number of hours it will take them to file N cards is   14._____

    A. $\dfrac{N}{\dfrac{N}{M} + \dfrac{N}{T}}$
    B. $\dfrac{N}{T+M} + \dfrac{2N}{MT}$
    C. $N\left(\dfrac{M}{N} + \dfrac{N}{T}\right)$
    D. $\dfrac{N}{NT + MN}$

Questions 15-20.

DIRECTIONS: Questions 15 through 20 are to be answered SOLELY on the basis of the information contained in the five charts below which relate to Bureau X in a City Department. The Bureau has an office in each of the five boroughs.

NUMBER OF UNITS OF WORK PRODUCED IN
THE BUREAU PER YEAR

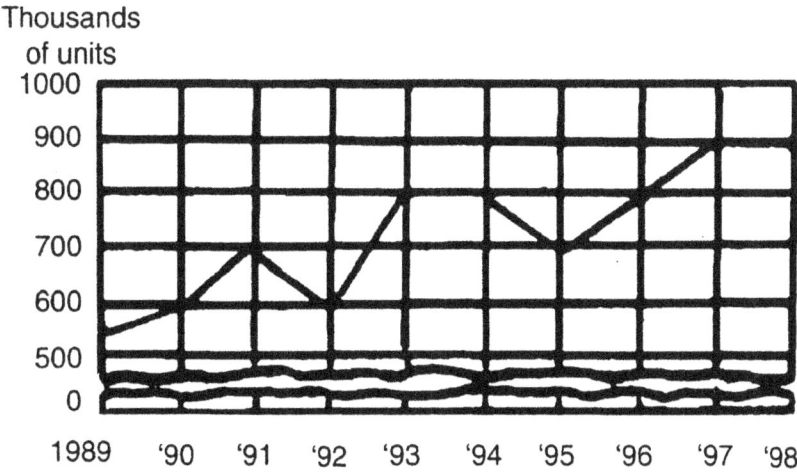

INCREASE IN THE NUMBER OF UNITS OF WORK PRODUCED IN 1998 OVER THE NUMBER PRODUCED IN 1989, BY BOROUGH

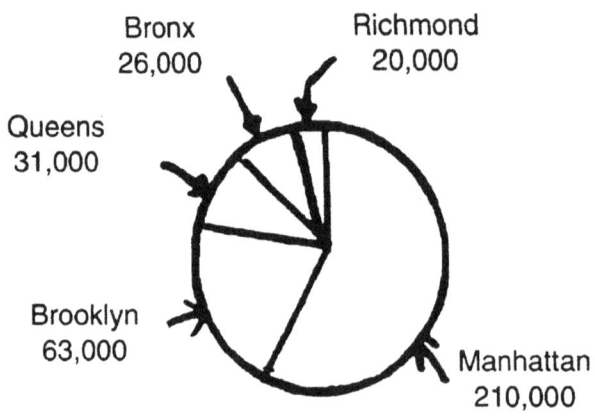

Bronx 26,000
Richmond 20,000
Queens 31,000
Brooklyn 63,000
Manhattan 210,000

NUMBER OF MALE AND FEMALE EMPLOYEES PRODUCING THE UNITS OF WORK THE BUREAU PER YEAR

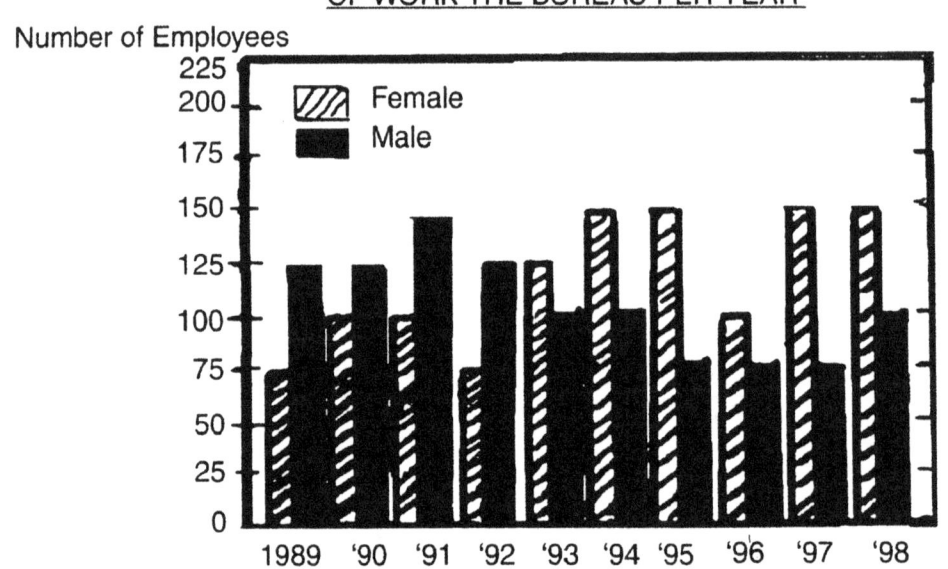

DISTRIBUTION OF THE AGES BY PER CENT, OF EMPLOYEES
ASSIGNED TO PRODUCE THE UNITS OF WORK IN THE YEARS
1989 AND 1998

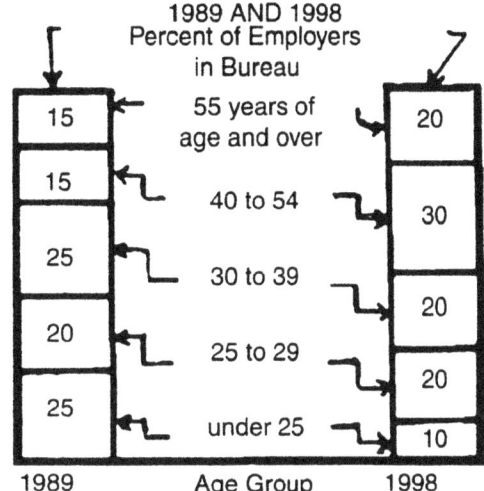

TOTAL SALARIES PAID PER YEAR TO EMPLOYEES ASSIGNED
TO PRODUCE THE UNITS OF WORK IN THE BUREAU

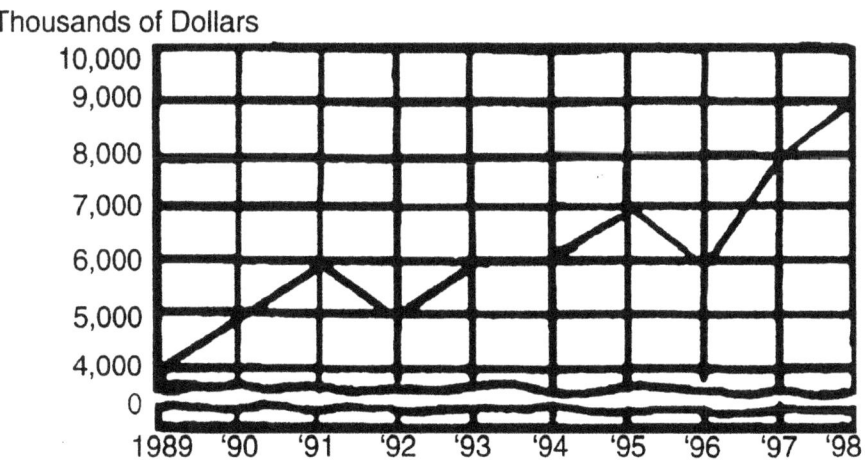

15. The information contained in the charts is sufficient to determine the 15.____

   A. amount of money paid in salaries to employees working in Richmond in 1998
   B. difference between the average annual salary of employees in the Bureau in 1998 and their average annual salary in 1997
   C. number of female employees in the Bureau between 30 and 39 years of age who were employed in 1989
   D. cost, in salary, for the average male employee in the Bureau to produce 100 units of work in 1994

16. The one of the following which was GREATER in the Bureau in 1994 than it was in 1992 was the

    A. cost, in salaries, of producing a unit of work
    B. units of work produced annually per employee
    C. proportion of female employees to total number of employees
    D. average annual salary per employee

17. If, in 1998, one-half of the employees in the Bureau 55 years of age and over each earned an annual salary of $42,000, then the average annual salary of all the remaining employees in the Bureau was MOST NEARLY

    A. $31,750   B. $34,500   C. $35,300   D. $35,800

18. Assume that, in 1989, the offices in Richmond and the Bronx each produced the same number of units of work. Also assume that, in 1989, the offices in Brooklyn, Manhattan, and Queens each produced twice as many units of work as were produced in either of the other two boroughs.
    Then, the number of units of work produced in Brooklyn in 1998 was MOST NEARLY

    A. 69,000   B. 138,000   C. 201,000   D. 225,000

19. If, in 1996, the average annual salary of the female employees in the Bureau was four-fifths as large as the average annual salary of the male employees, then the average annual salary of the female employees in that year was

    A. $37,500   B. $31,000   C. $30,500   D. $30,000

20. Of the total number of employees in the Bureau who were 30 years of age and over in 1989,

    A. at least 35 must have been females
    B. less than 75 must have been males
    C. no more than 100 must have been females
    D. more than 15 must have been males

KEY (CORRECT ANSWERS)

1.	D	11.	B
2.	C	12.	C
3.	D	13.	D
4.	A	14.	A
5.	B	15.	B
6.	B	16.	B
7.	C	17.	C
8.	B	18.	C
9.	A	19.	D
10.	D	20.	A

EXAMINATION SECTION
TEST 1

DIRECTIONS: Each question or incomplete statement is followed by several suggested answers or completions. Select the one that BEST answers the question or completes the statement. *PRINT THE LETTER OF THE CORRECT ANSWER IN THE SPACE AT THE RIGHT.*

1. The Public Services Careers Program is a manpower program

   A. designed to develop permanent employment opportunities for the disadvantaged
   B. designed to encourage college graduates to enter the field of public administration
   C. run by the federal government for private organizations
   D. designed to prepare physically handicapped persons for new positions

2. The Intergovernmental Personnel Act (P.L. 91-648) provides federal assistance to state and local governments for improving and strengthening personnel administration.
   The one of the following which is NOT provided for in this Act is

   A. creation of a new personnel system for upper-level personnel
   B. expanded training programs
   C. improved personnel management
   D. interchange of employees between federal government and state and local governments

3. Kepner-Tregoc management training courses are MOST closely involved with

   A. management by objectives
   B. development of overall leadership qualities
   C. leadership style
   D. problem-solving techniques

4. The BASIC purpose of the Managerial Grid for training program is to train managers to

   A. have concern for both production and the people who produce
   B. utilize scientific problem-solving techniques
   C. maximize efficient communication
   D. improve the quality of their leadership in *brainstorming* sessions

5. In establishing employee development objectives, management must make sure that they are

   A. stated in broad terms
   B. relevant to job performance
   C. developed by a training expert
   D. written in the vocabulary of the training field

6. In order that group conferences serve their purpose of developing professional staff, it is essential that

   A. discussion of controversial matters be limited
   B. notes be taken by the participants
   C. participants be encouraged to take part in the discussions
   D. chairmanships be rotated at the meetings

7. A personnel officer receives a request to conduct a course for interested employees who have filed for a promotion examination. The request that the course be given on agency time is turned down.
   This action is

   A. *justified;* such courses do not contain content that serve to improve employee performance
   B. *justified;* the course is designed to benefit the individual primarily, not the agency
   C. *unjustified;* regardless of objective, any training related to City operations will have an affect on employee performance tangibly or intangibly
   D. *unjustified;* if productivity has been based on full use of employee time, productivity will suffer if time is allocated for such a course

8. Of the following, the PRIMARY objective of sensitivity training is to

   A. teach management principles to participants
   B. improve and refine the decision-making process
   C. give the participants insight as to how they are perceived by others
   D. improve the emotional stability of the participants

9. In considering the functions of a manager, it is clear that the FIRST step in building a quality work force is the manager's need to

   A. design jobs to meet the realities of the labor market
   B. examine the qualification requirements for his positions and eliminate those which appear to be controversial
   C. determine the methods to be used in reaching that special public deemed most suitable for the agency
   D. establish controls so that there is reasonable assurance that the plans established to staff the agency will be properly consummated

10. Based on data documenting the differences between healthy and unhealthy organizations, which statement describes a healthy, as contrasted with an unhealthy, organization?

    A. Innovation is not widespread but exists in the hands of a few.
    B. Risks are not avoided but accepted as a condition of change.
    C. Decision-making is not dispersed but delegated to organizational levels.
    D. Conflict is not overt but resolved without confrontation.

11. Which of the following management actions is NOT conducive to greater job satisfaction?

    A. Diversifying tasks in the unit as much as feasible
    B. Permitting workers to follow through on tasks rather than carry out single segments of the process
    C. Avoiding the use of *project teams* or *task forces*
    D. Delegating authority to each layer of the hierarchy to the maximum extent possible

12. When the span of control of a manager or administrator is widened or increased, a MOST likely result is

    A. greater specificity of operational procedures
    B. a decrease in total worker-administrator contacts
    C. a blurring of objectives and goals
    D. an increase in responsibility of subordinates

12._____

13. Although *superagencies* may have value in assisting the chief executive to supervise operations more efficiently, a MAJOR shortcoming is that they

    A. may not provide more effective delivery of services to the public
    B. may limit the chief executive in his ability to find out what is happening within the agencies
    C. tend to reduce the responsibility of component agency heads for their own operations
    D. add costs that have little relation to the efforts to achieve administrative effectiveness

13._____

14. Business and psychological literature on managerial effectiveness is based for the MOST part on

    A. job analyses or descriptions about the management process
    B. field studies or observations about the outcome of effective management
    C. personal experiences or opinions about the traits good managers possess
    D. attitudes or perceptions of managers about organizational goals and strategies

14._____

15. The impression MOST likely to be gained from published surveys of traits necessary for management is that the lists

    A. limit identified traits to obvious human virtues
    B. lack precision in pinpointing behavioral elements
    C. emphasize negative rather than positive variables
    D. exclude attitudinal and motivational factors

15._____

16. Management concepts in public and private organizations have been undergoing drastic shifts as a consequence of a new view emerging from the recent synthesis of learning in the sciences. While still in its infancy, this development has challenged much of what has been considered accepted management theory for a long time.
    This change is frequently referred to in current management literature as

    A. systems thinking   B. scientific management
    C. behavioral science   D. multivariate analysis

16._____

17. Assuming more and more importance every day, the subject of management has undergone prodigious change in recent times.
    With respect to this development, the MOST valid expression concerning the current status of management would be:

    A. Authoritative texts have progressed to the point where differences in the formal treatment of the process of management are comparatively rare
    B. The generalized theory of management which has been synthesized recently by scholars in the field has given the term *management* a fixed meaning and definition from which revolutionary progress may now be anticipated
    C. Unity of conception, thought, and view about the process of management is still a long way off
    D. Unity of conception, thought, and view about the process of management has been achieved in administrative circles under the revolutionary concepts brought into being as a result of the latest developments in computer technology

18. That there is no average man, the manager would be first to acknowledge. Yet the exigencies of organized enterprise require that the assumption be made.
    Of the following, the procedure or process that is PRIMARILY based on this assumption is the

    A. administration of discipline
    B. establishment of rules and regulations
    C. policy of job enlargement
    D. promotion policy

19. There are four or more phases in the process of manpower planning.
    Of the following, the one which should be scheduled FIRST is

    A. gathering and analyzing data through manpower inventories and forecasts
    B. establishing objectives and policies through personnel and budget control units
    C. designing plan and action programs
    D. establishing production goals for the agency

20. When ranked in order of frequency of performance, studies show which of the following ranks LOWEST among the functions performed by central personnel offices in local governments?

    A. Planning, conducting, and coordinating training
    B. Certifying or auditing payrolls
    C. Conducting personnel investigations
    D. Engaging in collective bargaining

21. Which of the following activities of an agency personnel division can BEST be considered a control function?

    A. Scheduling safety meetings for supervisory staff
    B. Consultation on a disciplinary problem
    C. Reminders to line units to submit personnel evaluations
    D. Processing requests for merit increases

22. Which of the following interview styles is MOST appropriate for use in a problem-solving situation?   22.____

    A. Directed
    B. Non-directive
    C. Stress
    D. Authoritarian

23. Which of the following is a COMMONLY used measure of morale in an organization?   23.____

    A. Turnover rate
    B. Espirit de corps
    C. Specialized division of labor
    D. Job satisfaction

24. According to studies in personnel and industrial psychology, information that travels along the *grapevine* or informal communication system in an organization usually follows a pattern BEST classified as   24.____

    A. cluster—key informants tell several individuals, one of whom passes it on in the same way
    B. wheel—around through successive informants until it reaches the source
    C. chain—double informants linked to successive pairs
    D. random probability—informant tells anyone he happens to encounter, and so forth

25. A carefully devised program has been developed in a certain city for combining performance evaluation and seniority into a formula to determine order of layoff. The essence of this plan is first to group employees of a particular job class into *seniority blocks* and then to use performance evaluation as a basis for determining layoff order within each seniority block.   25.____
    The BEST of the following inferences which can be made from the above paragraph is that

    A. this plan is unfair since seniority is not given sufficient weight in the selection process
    B. this city is probably behind most civil service jurisdictions in the evaluation of employee performance
    C. combining performance and seniority cannot be done since it is like *combining apples and oranges*
    D. under this plan, it is conceivable that a person with high seniority could be laid off before a person with lower seniority

26. With any decentralization of personnel functions, specific procedures and rules are developed to assure conformance with relevant provisions of the Civil Service Law and the Rules and Regulations of the central personnel agency.   26.____
    To the extent that these procedures are specific and detailed,

    A. agency involvement in the execution of the decentralized function will be limited
    B. agency discretion in the administration of the decentralized function will be limited
    C. size and composition of agency personnel staff will tend to become fixed
    D. flexibility of application to bolster agency performance will be provided

27. While decentralization of personnel functions to give operating agencies more authority in personnel matters relating to their operations has been a goal of personnel policy, recentralization is an ever-present possibility. Of the following, the factor which is the BEST indicator of the desirability of recentralization is that

   A. inconsistent policies or inconsistent application of policies resulted when decentralized operations were instituted
   B. costs in terms of personnel and procedures increased significantly when decentralization was introduced
   C. the decentralization did not serve any real identifiable need
   D. agency personnel units were not prepared to handle the responsibilities delegated to them

28. Although the Department of Personnel has developed and maintains an Executive Roster, its use by agency heads to fill managerial positions has been disappointing.
Of the following, the one that is the LEAST likely reason for NOT using the roster is that

   A. personal factors essential to the relationship of manager and administrator are not revealed in the roster record
   B. most agencies prefer to advance their own employees rather than use a general roster
   C. some agency heads think of experienced City managerial employees as superannuated administrative deadwood
   D. use of the roster implies a reduction of the scope of administrative discretion in selection

29. During one program year, an examiner found a number of occasions in which a special task, a special report, or some activity outside of planned programs had to be assigned. One staff member continually offered to undertake these assignments whenever the administrative examiner requested a volunteer. He handled these jobs in timely fashion even though he had begun the year with a full-time workload.
Of the following, the conclusion MOST warranted from the information given is that the

   A. staff member was much more efficient than other examiners in the division in planning and executing work
   B. staff member's regular workload actually was less than a full-time assignment for him
   C. commitment and will to serve was greater in this member than in others
   D. quality of work of other examiners may have been higher than that of this staff member

30. An examiner has three subordinate supervisors, each responsible for a major program in his division. He finds that one supervisor is much weaker than the other two, both in his planning of work and in his follow-through to achieve timely completion of tasks. To bolster the *weak* supervisor, the administrative examiner reassigns his best examiners to this unit.
This decision is POOR primarily because

   A. the performance of the competent examiners is likely to suffer eventually
   B. the assigned examiners will be expected to make more decisions themselves
   C. the ineffective supervisor might have done better by assignment elsewhere
   D. indicated disciplinary action was not taken

31. Because of the frustrations felt by many public administrators who have been unable to motivate their subordinates, the classic civil service reform movement has been condemned by observers of the public government scene. Those condemning that movement believe that the system has failed to develop a quality public service precisely because of the policies implemented as a result of the reform movement.
They suggest that the remedy lies in

    A. centralizing the personnel functions in the hands of an elite group of professional personnel practitioners who would be best equipped to initiate needed remedies
    B. changing the concept of personnel management to a generalist approach, thus guaranteeing a broader and more integrated resolution of employee problems
    C. finding and implementing more practical personnel techniques in dealing with the various functional personnel areas
    D. completely decentralizing personnel administration to the responsible agency heads

31._____

32. The British scholar and statesman Harold J. Laski has stated that the expert was too likely to *make his subject the measure of life, instead of making life the measure of his subject.*
When applying this comment to the modern public service administrator, it is meant that the administrator should

    A. expand the jurisdiction of his authority so that better integration among functional areas is possible
    B. personally be receptive to the concept of change and not merely concerned with protecting the methods of the past
    C. develop a group of specialists in functional subject matter areas in order to give better service to the operating department heads
    D. see the relationship of his own particular area of jurisdiction to other governmental activities and to the private sector

32._____

33. Suppose that, as an examiner, you are asked to prepare a budget for the next fiscal year for a division performing personnel functions.
Of the following, the consideration which is LEAST important to your development of the division budget involves

    A. adequacy of the current year's budget for your division
    B. changes in workload that can be anticipated
    C. budget restrictions that have been indicated in a memorandum covering budget preparation
    D. staff reassignments which are expected during that fiscal year

33._____

34. Suppose you have been designated chairman of an intra-departmental committee to implement a major policy decision. The one of the following which is LEAST desirable as a subject for a planning meeting is

    A. determination of details of execution by each bureau
    B. specific allocation of responsibility for the phases of administration
    C. provision of means for coordination and follow-up
    D. formulation of sub-goals for each bureau

35. Collective bargaining challenges the concept of the neutrality of the personnel function in the public service. Which one of the following statements BEST reflects this observation?

    A. Personnel offices must clearly serve as a bridge between management and employees.
    B. In most cases, negotiation involves a tripartite group—labor relations, fiscal or budget, and the employee organization.
    C. Personnel bureaus must be identified openly with the public employer.
    D. Personnel units cannot make policy or commitments in labor relations; their primary function is to execute personnel decisions made by others.

36. Changes in the field of public employee labor relations have been both numerous and significant in recent years. Below are four statements that an examiner preparing a report on developments in this area of personnel management might possibly include as correct:

    I. At least one-third of the states give some type of bargaining rights to their employees
    II. Less than half the states have granted public employees the right to organize
    III. Since 1959, at least eight states have enacted comprehensive labor relations laws affecting public employees
    IV. By 1966, state and local governments had entered into more than 1,000 separate agreements with employee organizations

    Which of the following choices lists the statements that are CORRECT?

    A. I, II, and III are correct, but not IV
    B. I, III, and IV are correct, but not II
    C. I and III are correct, but not II and IV
    D. II and III are correct, but not I and IV

37. Which of the following is NOT a major goal of unions in contract negotiations?

    A. Establishing management prerogatives
    B. Preserving and strengthening the union
    C. Promoting social and economic objectives
    D. Promoting the status of the union representatives

Questions 38-39.

DIRECTIONS: Answer Questions 38 and 39 on the basis of the following paragraph.

An impending reorganization within an agency will mean loss by transfer of several professional staff members from the personnel division. The division chief is asked to designate the persons to be transferred. After reviewing the implications of this reduction of staff with his assistant, the division chief discussed the matter at a staff meeting. He adopts the recommendations of several staff members to have volunteers make up the required reduction.

38. The decision to permit personnel to volunteer for transfer is 38.____

   A. *poor;* it is not likely that the members of a division are of equal value to the division chief
   B. *good;* dissatisfied members will probably be more productive elsewhere
   C. *poor;* the division chief has abdicated his responsibility to carry out the order given to him
   D. *good;* morale among remaining staff is likely to improve in a more cohesive framework

39. Suppose one of the volunteers is a recently appointed employee who has completed his probationary period acceptably, but whose attitude toward division operations and agency administration tends to be rather negative and sometimes even abrasive. Because of his lack of commitment to the division, his transfer is recommended. If the transfer is approved, the division chief should, prior to the transfer, 39.____

   A. discuss with the staff the importance of commitment to the work of the agency and its relationship with job satisfaction
   B. refrain from any discussion of attitude with the employee
   C. discuss with the employee his concern about the employee's attitude
   D. avoid mention of attitude in the evaluation appraisal prepared for the receiving division chief

40. It is time to make position classification a real help to line officials in defining programs and objectives and structuring tasks to meet those objectives, rather than continuing to act as a post auditor and controller. 40.____
   Of the following, the statement which BEST reflects the sense of this passage is that

   A. post audit and control procedures should be related to the prior processes of objectives and goals determination
   B. position classification should be part of management decisions rather than an evaluation of them
   C. program definition requires prior determination of position characteristics and performance factors to facilitate management program decisions
   D. primary responsibility for position classification and grade or level allocation is that of line management, not that of the classification specialist

41. Pencil and paper objective testing procedures have tremendous advantages of quantification and empiricism. They are economical in production and use. But the procedures have a great disadvantage in that they are designed primarily for statistical prediction.
A conclusion that is MOST consistent with the above statement is that

   A. statistical prediction becomes meaningless if the applicants tested constitute a stratified sample and not a representative sample of the population
   B. predictions of adequate performance by any one group of successful applicants will follow the normal curve
   C. if the group is small, statistical indices cannot have high validity
   D. such test procedures cannot predict the job success or failure of a specific applicant

42. It has been stated that in the public service, the use of written tests is more appropriate for selecting from among those outside the organization than from those within the organization.
This is so since

   A. written tests serve to reduce the number of final competitors to manageable proportions
   B. vouchering of prospective employees from outside the organization is deemed to be invalid and not reliable
   C. written tests are in effect substitutes for direct observation on the gob
   D. testing outside applicants for aptitude and achievement has served a useful purpose in the elimination of extraneous prejudicial factors in the selection process

43. The *Test Validation Board* is a recent innovation.
The MAJOR purpose of this board is to review

   A. and approve questions to be used before the written test is held
   B. and approve the test questions and the proposed key answers immediately after the test is held
   C. the test items and protests and then establish the final key answers
   D. the test items and protests and then recommend adoption of a final rating key

44. *Brainstorming* sessions include each of the following EXCEPT

   A. free-wheeling or wild ideas
   B. criticism of any idea
   C. great quantities of ideas
   D. combining or building on ideas

45. It has been ascertained that a certain top-level position should NOT be placed in the competitive class.
What determines whether the new position should be placed in the non-competitive class rather than in the exempt class?

   A. Subordinate positions are in the competitive class.
   B. An executive in a specific field is needed.
   C. The position can be subjected to examination.
   D. The position is policy making.

46. Personnel practice in most governmental organizations provides that a new employee must serve a probationary period generally not to exceed six months. During this period, he is to be given special attention in such matters as instruction, indoctrination, and general adjustment to his job. The theory behind this practice is that this period is the last phase of the testing process, but the consensus is that the probationary period is not living up to its possibilities as a testing opportunity.
   The MAJOR reason for this opinion is that the

   A. techniques used by personnel practitioners to encourage supervisors to pass objective judgments on probationers are not effective
   B. probationary period is too short and marginal employees can maintain their best behavior for this length of time
   C. supervisors are not living up to their obligation to conduct vigorous probationary appraisals
   D. supervisors try to avoid making unpleasant personal judgments about their employees

46.____

47. Plans were recently announced to require one year of college for entrance into the police service and eventually a college degree for promotion in the police force.
   Of the following, the one that will NOT present problems in implementing these plans is

   A. changing the Civil Service requirements for entrance or promotion
   B. overcoming police union objections to the promotion requirements
   C. providing sufficient time for affected individuals to meet these educational requirements
   D. retaining college graduates in the police service over a period of years

47.____

Questions 48–50.

DIRECTIONS: Answer Questions 48 through 50 on the basis of the following paragraph.

The increase in the extent to which each individual is personally responsible to others is most noticeable in a large bureaucracy. No one person decides anything; each decision of any importance is the product of an intricate process of brokerage involving individuals inside and outside the organization who feel some reason to be affected by the decision, or who have special knowledge to contribute to it. The more varied the organization's constituency, the more outside "veto-groups" will need to be taken into account. But even if no outside consultations were involved, sheer size would produce a complex process of decision. For a large organization is a deliberately created system of tensions into which each individual is expected to bring work–ways, viewpoints, and outside relationships markedly different from those of his colleagues. It is the administrator's task to draw from these disparate forces the elements of wise action from day to day, consistent with the purposes of the organization as a whole.

48. This passage is ESSENTIALLY a description of decision-making as

   A. an organization process
   B. the key responsibility of the administrator
   C. the one best position among many
   D. a complex of individual decisions

48.____

49. Which one of the following statements BEST describes the responsibilities of an administrator?
    He

    A. modifies decisions and goals in accordance with pressures from within and outside the organization
    B. creates problem-solving mechanisms that rely on the varied interests of his staff and *veto-groups*
    C. makes determinations that will lead to attainment of his agency's objectives
    D. obtains agreement among varying viewpoints and interests

50. In the context of the operations of a central public personnel agency, a *veto-group* would LEAST likely consist of

    A. employee organizations
    B. professional personnel societies
    C. using agencies
    D. civil service newspapers

KEY (CORRECT ANSWERS)

1. A	11. C	21. C	31. D	41. D
2. A	12. D	22. B	32. D	42. C
3. D	13. A	23. A	33. D	43. D
4. A	14. C	24. A	34. A	44. B
5. B	15. B	25. D	35. C	45. B
6. C	16. A	26. B	36. B	46. C
7. B	17. C	27. C	37. A	47. C
8. C	18. B	28. D	38. A	48. A
9. A	19. A	29. B	39. C	49. C
10. B	20. D	30. A	40. B	50. B

TEST 2

DIRECTIONS: Each question or incomplete statement is followed by several suggested answers or completions. Select the one that BEST answers the question or completes the statement. *PRINT THE LETTER OF THE CORRECT ANSWER IN THE SPACE AT THE RIGHT.*

1. The definition of merit system as it pertains to the public service is that a person's worth to the organization is the factor governing both his entrance and upward mobility within that service. The main ingredient used to accomplish entrance and mobility has been competition based on relative qualifications of candidates.
The burgeoning demands of new occupations and critical social and economic urgencies in the public service make it imperative that now

    A. greater emphasis be placed on the intellectual and technical capacities of applicants in order to improve the high standards achieved by some professionals
    B. current methods be strengthened in order to make them more valid and reliable indicators among applicants for government positions
    C. public personnel officials work more closely with representatives of the various professions and occupations to establish more equitable minimum standards in order to improve the quality of its practitioners
    D. the system adapt to the new changes by establishing alternative methods more suitable to current needs

1.____

2. Civil service systems need to be reexamined from time to time to determine whether they are correctly fulfilling stated merit obligations. Frequently, inspection determines that what was once a valid practice ... has ceased to be an effective instrument and has become, instead, an unrealistic barrier to the implementation of merit principles. Which one of the following practices would be considered to be such an unrealistic barrier?

    A. Disqualifying candidates with poor work history for positions involving the operation of trains or buses
    B. Disqualifying candidates for police work who have records of serious arrests
    C. Requiring a degree or license for medical, scientific, and professional positions
    D. Requiring a high school diploma for custodial, maintenance, and service positions

2.____

3. It is generally accepted that work attitudes and interpersonal relationships contribute at least as much as knowledge and ability to job performance. Several personality measuring and appraisal devices have been found useful in predicting personality and work attitudes.
A MAJOR drawback in their use in competitive selection, however, is the

    A. *fakeability* of responses possible in such selection situations
    B. cost of the materials and their interpretation
    C. inability of these measures to predict actual job performance
    D. lack of reviewability of these devices

3.____

4. Human Relations School discoveries having a major impact on modern personnel practices include all of the following EXCEPT that

   A. social as well as physical capacity determines the amount of work an employee does
   B. non-economic rewards play a central role in employee motivation
   C. the higher the degree of specialization, the more efficient the division of labor
   D. workers react to management as members of groups rather than as individuals

5. Studies of the relationship between creativity and intelligence indicate that creativity

   A. is one of several special intelligence factors
   B. consists primarily of general intelligence as measured by standardized tests
   C. involves non-intellective factors as well as minimums of intelligence
   D. relates more directly to quantitative than to verbal aptitudes and skills

6. Strategies of data collection applicable to personnel work can be grouped into two broad categories: the mechanical method in which data be collected according to pre-established guidelines, rules, or procedures, and the clinical method in which the manner of data collection may differ from candidate to candidate at the discretion of the professional person collecting it.
   An argument that has proved VALID in support of the clinical method is that

   A. no sound basis exists for writing any single set of rules for collecting data
   B. no known mechanical procedure can fully anticipate all potentially relevant data
   C. mechanical processes stress the use of techniques such as synthetic validation
   D. mechanical methods are inadequate for formulating optimal individualized prediction rules

7. Which one of the following actions appears LEAST mandated by the Griggs vs. Duke Power Company decision of the U.S. Supreme Court on discriminatory employment practice?

   A. Study of certification and appointment policies and procedures
   B. Determination of job performance standards as related to successful performance
   C. Review of personal history forms, applications, and interviews involved in employment procedures
   D. Test validation by correlation of individual test items with total test scores

8. In decision-making terminology, the type of action taken on a problem when the decision-maker finds that he cannot do anything to eliminate the cause is MOST often called _____ action.

   A. corrective   B. adaptive
   C. stopgap   D. interim

9. The Intergovernmental Personnel Act became law recently. This Act does NOT provide for

   A. temporary assignment of personnel between governmental jurisdiction
   B. grants for improving personnel administration and training
   C. interstate compacts for personnel and training activities
   D. a National Advisory Council to study federal personnel administration and make recommendations to the President and Congress

10. Following are three kinds of performance tests for which arrangements might be made to give the candidates a pretest warm-up period:
    I. typing
    II. truck driving
    III. stenography

    Which one of the following choices lists all of the above tests that should be preceded by a warm-up session?

    A. I, III
    B. II *only*
    C. I, II, III
    D. None of the above

Questions 11–12.

DIRECTIONS: Answer Questions 11 and 12 on the basis of the following paragraph.

Your role as human resources utilization experts is to submit your techniques to operating administrators, for the program must in reality be theirs, not yours. We in personnel have been guilty of encouraging operating executives to believe that these important matters affecting their employees are personnel department matters, not management matters. We should hardly be surprised, as a consequence, to find these executives playing down the role of personnel and finding personnel "routines" a nuisance, for these are not in the mainstream of managing the enterprise—or so we have encouraged them to believe.

11. The BEST of the following interpretations of the above paragraph is that

    A. personnel people have been guilty of *passing the buck* on personnel functions
    B. operating officials have difficulty understanding personnel techniques
    C. personnel employees have tended to usurp some functions rightfully belonging to management
    D. matters affecting employees should be handled by the personnel department

12. The BEST of the following interpretations of the above paragraph is that

    A. personnel departments have aided and abetted the formulation of negative attitudes on the part of management
    B. personnel people are labor relations experts and should carry out these duties
    C. personnel activities are not really the responsibility of management
    D. management is now being encouraged by personnel experts to assume some responsibility for personnel functions

13. Employee training can be described BEST as a process that

    A. increases retention of skills
    B. changes employees' knowledge, skills, or aptitudes
    C. improves the work methods used
    D. improves the work environment

14. With respect to the use of on-the-job training methods, the theory is that it is possible to create maximally favorable conditions for learning while on the job. In actual practice, it has been found that these favorable conditions are difficult to achieve.
    The MAIN reason militating against such ideal conditions is that

    A. the primary function on the job is production, and training must, therefore, take second place
    B. an adequate number of skilled and knowledgeable employees is usually not available to engage in effective person-to-person training
    C. expensive equipment and work space are tied up during training, which is not advantageous to establishing good rapport between trainer and trainee
    D. an appraisal of trainee learning under pressure of job demands is not conducive to showing the trainee the reasons for his mistakes

15. In most major studies directed toward identification of productive scientific personnel, the MOST effective predictor has been

    A. biographical information
    B. motivational analysis
    C. tests of ideational flexibility
    D. high-level reasoning tests

16. Because interviewing is a difficult art, MOST personnel people who conduct interviews

    A. break the interview into specific units with pauses in between
    B. remain fairly constant in the technique they use despite differences of purpose and persons interviewed
    C. utilize non-directive techniques during their first few years of interviewing
    D. vary their style and technique in accordance with the purpose of the interview and the personality of the persons interviewed

17. When using the *in-basket* technique, it is NOT possible to obtain measures of the

    A. amount of work done in a given time
    B. extent to which the candidate seeks guidance before making decisions
    C. proportion of decisions that lead to actual cost savings
    D. proportion of work time devoted to prepatory activities

18. The MOST appropriate people to develop the definition for specific classes of positions in order that they may serve as useful criteria for allocating positions to classes are the

    A. personnel experts in the area of job evaluation
    B. program practitioners
    C. job analysts working within other occupations under study
    D. organization and methods analysts

19. By its very nature and in order to operate effectively, a job classification system which groups jobs into broad occupational categories and then subdivides them into levels of difficulty and responsibility requires

    A. the upgrading of positions in order to raise the pay rates of incumbents
    B. a process in which lengthy job descriptions covering the allocation criteria are prerequisites
    C. a certain amount of central control
    D. the transfer of classification authority from an *inside-track priesthood to* the operating official

20. A plan of classifying positions based on duties and responsibilities is not the same thing as a pay plan. Although the classification arrangement may be a vital element upon which a compensation structure is based and administered, there are differences between the two plans. The MAJOR distinction between these plans can be illustrated best by the fact that

    A. a uniform accounting system requires a uniform job terminology, which can be accomplished best by a classification plan
    B. the compensation plan can be changed without affecting the classification plan, and classes of positions can be rearranged on a pay schedule without changing the schedule
    C. job evaluation results in a common understanding of the job for which a rate is being set and for job-to-job comparison
    D. the classification principle of *equal pay for equal work* was instrumental in evolving pay reform

21. By stretching higher grade duties over as many jobs as possible, the position classifier makes for

    A. economy
    B. more effective performance
    C. effective use of the labor market
    D. higher operational costs

22. Contemporary information about what people want that is pertinent to potential entrants to the public service labor market indicates that a MAJOR want is

    A. more time for play and less time for work
    B. more personal privacy and fewer creature comforts
    C. more employee relationships and less organizational hierarchy
    D. more political participation and less partisan neutrality

23. An occupational rather than an organizational commitment to personnel administration as a professional field is MOST likely to prevail among personnel workers who perceive their work as part of a function that is

    A. designed to serve the employees of their agency
    B. dominated by necessary but uninteresting tasks
    C. dedicated to obtaining compliance with the law
    D. devoted to the human problems of organizations

24. The FIRST major strike by city employees which tested the Condon-Wadlin Act was by employees of the

    A. Sanitation Department
    B. Police Department
    C. Fire Department
    D. Department of Welfare

25. In the aftermath of the city transit strike of 1966, study groups were appointed to recommend ways in which such strikes could be avoided.
    The recommendations made at that time by the Governor's Committee and the American Arbitration Association were especially significant in that they both

    A. included machinery for the settlement of labor disputes which was to be set up outside the regular civil service establishment
    B. advocated the retention of the legal prohibition against strikes by public employees
    C. agreed to imposition of heavy fines on the union in case of a strike
    D. opted for repeal of the section in the Condon-Wadlin Act which prohibited strikes

26. Of the following, which country was the pioneer in employee-management relationships within the public service?

    A. Canada   B. France   C. Australia   D. Mexico

27. There are notable similarities and differences between collective bargaining in industry and government.
    In which of the following areas are the similarities GREATEST?

    A. Negotiable subjects
    B. Bargaining processes
    C. Mediation and arbitration
    D. Strikes

28. Traditionally, white-collar and professional workers resisted unionization both in government and in industry. This attitude has changed drastically among these workers since the late 1950's, however, particularly among public employees.
    The BASIC cause behind this change among public employees was that

    A. organized labor trained its big union recruitment guns on organizing these workers in the face of the dwindling proportion of blue-collar people in the labor force
    B. these employees generally identified with middle-class America, which had now become union-oriented
    C. they felt deep frustration with the authoritarianism of public administrators who believed that the *merit system* process gave the employee all the protection he needed
    D. the continual upward spiral of inflation resulted in making these workers among those deemed economically disadvantaged and necessitated their joining in unions for their own protection

29. Union efforts to improve retirement benefits for public employees have caused concern in the State legislature. Recently, a special legislative committee was ordered to determine whether retirement benefits should remain a subject for collective bargaining or whether they should be regulated by

    A. a bipartisan pension commission
    B. a board designated by management and labor
    C. large commercial insurance carriers
    D. the State Insurance Fund

30. The performance of personnel functions which are part of a comprehensive and integrated program of personnel management is conditioned significantly by personnel policies. Which one of the following is the LEAST valid criterion of what positive policies can accomplish?

    A. Functions are governed by rules which permit their being performed in line with the desired goals of the organization.
    B. Guidance for executives restrains them from mishandling the specified functions with which they have been entrusted.
    C. Standard decisions make it unnecessary for subordinates to ask their supervisors how given problems should be handled.
    D. Goals are enunciated for the purpose of selecting candidates best equipped to prove successful in the particular organizational milieu.

31. The GREATEST handicap of personnel systems which are predicated on the *corps of people* concept rather than on job analysis is lack of facility for

    A. conducting program evaluation studies
    B. developing sound programs for the direction and control of productivity
    C. manpower planning
    D. determining the limits of authority and responsibility among managerial personnel

32. It is an anomaly that one of the greatest threats to maintaining classification plans adequately is slowness in adjusting salaries to keep up with the changing labor market. Thus, distortions of many classification plans occur.
    This is MAINLY due to

    A. pressure from management officials to upgrade employees who have not received salary range increases
    B. inability to maintain an adequate file of pertinent pay data
    C. conflict in the pay philosophy between maintaining external alignment and comparability with union rates
    D. difficulty in distinguishing between the pay program and the fringe benefit package

33. A personnel agency charged with identifying candidates with the kind of creative talent that can be used in an organizational setting should look for a high degree of certain attributes among the candidate population. Below are listed four characteristics which may qualify as desirable attributes for the purpose indicated:
    I. Self-confidence
    II. Social conformity
    III. Mobility aspirations
    IV. Job involvement

    Which of the following choices lists ALL of the above attributes which the personnel agency should look for?

    A. I, II, IV
    B. I, III, IV
    C. II, III, IV
    D. III, IV

34. With regard to educational standards for selection purposes, the U.S. Supreme Court has held that such requirements should be

    A. eliminated in most cases
    B. related to job success
    C. maintained whenever possible
    D. reduced as far as possible

35. In surveying job series which would be most conducive to job restructuring, most attention has focused on P, T, and M positions.
    The benefits claimed for job restructuring include all of the following EXCEPT

    A. creating more interesting and challenging P, T, and M jobs
    B. increasing promotional opportunities for P, T, and M employees
    C. providing more job opportunities for the lesser skilled
    D. creating new promotional opportunities for those in low-skill or dead-end jobs

36. We must restructure as many job series as possible to allow entry into the service and to permit successful job performance without previous training and experience. In the type of restructuring alluded to, it is ESSENTIAL that

    A. job duties be rearranged to form a learning progression as well as a means of reaching work objectives
    B. educational achievement be minimized as a factor in determining progression to higher position rank
    C. separate and distinctive job series be created independent of existing job series
    D. lateral entry opportunities be emphasized

37. From the standpoint of equal opportunity, the MOST critical item operating personnel must focus on is

    A. hiring more minority applicants for top-level positions
    B. helping existing minority employees upgrade their skills so they may qualify for higher skilled positions
    C. placing minority candidates in job categories where, there is little minority representation
    D. eliminating merit system principles

38. Most of the jobs opened up in human services through new career development efforts have been filled by women.
Of the following, the MAIN reason for this result is that the

    A. need to develop suitable careers for women is the major focus of the program
    B. majority of new career jobs are in fields where the work normally has been done by women
    C. labor shortages are found in fields that draw heavily on womanpower
    D. legislation and funds provide guides which emphasize the employment of women who are disadvantaged or underemployed

38.____

39. Thirty years ago, the Federal District Court granted a preliminary injunction restraining the city school system's board of examiners from conducting supervisory examinations or issuing lists based on them.
The reason given for this judicial action was that the

    A. disadvantaged and minority group members were given preferential treatment
    B. eligibility requirements were too high
    C. rating used was based on a *pass–fail* scoring system
    D. tests discriminated against Blacks and Puerto Ricans

39.____

40. The city recently began making thousands of jobs available to the unemployed and underemployed. This program, administered by the Human Resources Administration, implements the Federal Emergency Employment Act.
The federal statute provides that FIRST priority for such jobs be given to

    A. heads of households
    B. persons living alone
    C. veterans of the Indochina or Korean War
    D. youths entering the labor market

40.____

41. According to the Equal Employment Opportunity Act of 1966, a covered employer may NOT

    A. discriminate against an individual because he is a member of the Communist Party in the United States
    B. indicate preference for or limitation to national origin in printing a notice or advertisement for employment
    C. employ only members of a certain religion if the employer is an educational institution owned or supported by that religion
    D. apply different pay scales, conditions, or facilities of employment according to the location of various plants or facilities

41.____

42. Data received by the Equal Employment Opportunity Commission from firms employing 100 or more people suggest that emphasis in the area of equal opportunity has shifted from one of detection of conscious discrimination to one of

    A. human resources utilization
    B. passive resistance
    C. unconscious discrimination
    D. education

42.____

43. According to surveys pertaining to equal employment opportunities, available information indicates that discriminatory patterns in job placement of minority group members is

    A. higher in craft unions than in industrial unions
    B. greater in the East than in the West
    C. higher in new plants than in old plants
    D. higher among young executives than among old executives

44. The area of criticism on which Congress concentrated its attention in its recent investigations of testing was

    A. cultural bias
    B. depersonalization of the individual
    C. increase in *meritocracy*
    D. invasion of privacy

45. If accepted criteria of a profession are applied, which of the following work groupings ranks LOWEST in the distinctiveness of its character as a profession?

    A. Social service or community work
    B. Managerial or administrative work
    C. Health or health services work
    D. Teaching or educational work

46. Surveys of factors contributing to job satisfaction indicate, according to employees, that the factor having HIGHEST priority among those listed is

    A. opportunity for advancement
    B. good pay schedules
    C. concern for training employees for better job performance
    D. good work environment

47. Job enrichment is intended to increase employee motivation and interest by increasing the accountability of employees for their work, by introducing more complex tasks, and by granting authority to make job decisions.
    A MAJOR hazard that may result from application of such restructuring is to

    A. increase complaints of work pressure
    B. reduce the effectiveness of task specialization
    C. stimulate demand for salary increases
    D. limit the status of the immediate supervisor

48. Which of the following statements concerning performance appraisal systems is NOT correct?
    They

    A. require line management participation
    B. provide for periodic discussions of performance between the supervisor and the employee
    C. are used primarily to uncover employee weaknesses
    D. require supervisor training to assure uniform appraisals

49. In the forced-choice technique of performance evaluation, the rater is forced to judge which of several alternative statements is most descriptive of an employee's performance. It forces the rater to discriminate on the basis of concrete aspects of a subordinate's work behavior rather than to rely on an impression of his total worth.
The one of the following which is NOT considered a value of this technique is that it

   A. increases rater ability to produce a desired outcome
   B. is relatively free of the usual pile-up at the top of the scale
   C. tends to minimize subjective elements
   D. produces results that correlate positively with other variables associated with effective job performance

50. Of the following, the one which is NOT an advantage of the proper delegation of work by a manager is that it

   A. increases planning time
   B. relieves the tension of seeing to details
   C. increases the manager's familiarity with routine work
   D. increases understanding of the responsibilities of subordinates

KEY (CORRECT ANSWERS)

1. D	11. C	21. D	31. C	41. B
2. D	12. A	22. C	32. A	42. A
3. A	13. B	23. D	33. B	43. A
4. C	14. A	24. D	34. B	44. D
5. C	15. D	25. A	35. B	45. B
6. B	16. B	26. A	36. A	46. A
7. D	17. C	27. B	37. B	47. D
8. B	18. A	28. C	38. B	48. C
9. D	19. C	29. A	39. D	49. A
10. C	20. B	30. D	40. C	50. C

PHILOSOPHY, PRINCIPLES, PRACTICES, AND TECHNICS OF SUPERVISION, ADMINISTRATION, MANAGEMENT, AND ORGANIZATION

TABLE OF CONTENTS

	Page
MEANING OF SUPERVISION	1
THE OLD AND THE NEW SUPERVISION	1
THE EIGHT (8) BASIC PRINCIPLES OF THE NEW SUPERVISION	1
I. Principle of Responsibility	1
II. Principle of Authority	2
III. Principle of Self-Growth	2
IV. Principle of Individual Worth	2
V. Principle of Creative Leadership	2
VI. Principle of Success and Failure	2
VII. Principle of Science	3
VIII. Principle of Cooperation	3
WHAT IS ADMINISTRATION?	3
I. Practices Commonly Classed as "Supervisory"	3
II. Practices Commonly Classed as "Administrative"	3
III. Practices Commonly Classed as Both "Supervisory" and "Administrative"	4
RESPONSIBILITIES OF THE SUPERVISOR	4
COMPETENCIES OF THE SUPERVISOR	4
THE PROFESSIONAL SUPERVISOR-EMPLOYEE RELATIONSHIP	4
MINI-TEXT IN SUPERVISION, ADMINISTRATION, MANAGEMENT, AND ORGANIZATION	5
I. Brief Highlights	5
A. Levels of Management	6
B. What the Supervisor Must Learn	6
C. A Definition of Supervision	6
D. Elements of the Team Concept	6
E. Principles of Organization	6
F. The Four Important Parts of Every Job	7
G. Principles of Delegation	7
H. Principles of Effective Communications	7
I. Principles of Work Improvement	7
J. Areas of Job Improvement	7
K. Seven Key Points in Making Improvements	8

	L.	Corrective Techniques for Job Improvement	8
	M.	A Planning Checklist	8
	N.	Five Characteristics of Good Directions	9
	O.	Types of Directions	9
	P.	Controls	9
	Q.	Orienting the New Employee	9
	R.	Checklist for Orienting New Employees	9
	S.	Principles of Learning	10
	T.	Causes of Poor Performance	10
	U.	Four Major Steps in On-the-Job Instructions	10
	V.	Employees Want Five Things	10
	W.	Some Don'ts in Regard to Praise	11
	X.	How to Gain Your Workers' Confidence	11
	Y.	Sources of Employee Problems	11
	Z.	The Supervisor's Key to Discipline	11
	AA.	Five Important Processes of Management	12
	BB.	When the Supervisor Fails to Plan	12
	CC.	Fourteen General Principles of Management	12
	DD.	Change	12
II.	Brief Topical Summaries		13
	A.	Who/What is the Supervisor?	13
	B.	The Sociology of Work	13
	C.	Principles and Practices of Supervision	14
	D.	Dynamic Leadership	14
	E.	Processes for Solving Problems	15
	F.	Training for Results	15
	G.	Health, Safety, and Accident Prevention	16
	H.	Equal Employment Opportunity	16
	I.	Improving Communications	16
	J.	Self-Development	17
	K.	Teaching and Training	17
		1. The Teaching Process	17
		a. Preparation	17
		b. Presentation	18
		c. Summary	18
		d. Application	18
		e. Evaluation	18
		2. Teaching Methods	18
		a. Lecture	18
		b. Discussion	18
		c. Demonstration	19
		d. Performance	19
		e. Which Method to Use	19

PHILOSOPHY, PRINCIPLES, PRACTICES, AND TECHNICS OF SUPERVISION, ADMINISTRATION, MANAGEMENT, AND ORGANIZATION

MEANING OF SUPERVISION

The extension of the democratic philosophy has been accompanied by an extension in the scope of supervision. Modern leaders and supervisors no longer think of supervision in the narrow sense of being confined chiefly to visiting employees, supplying materials, or rating the staff. They regard supervision as being intimately related to all the concerned agencies of society, they speak of the supervisor's function in terms of "growth," rather than the "improvement" of employees.

This modern concept of supervision may be defined as follows: Supervision is leadership and the development of leadership within groups which are cooperatively engaged in inspection, research, training, guidance, and evaluation.

THE OLD AND THE NEW SUPERVISION

TRADITIONAL
1. Inspection
2. Focused on the employee
3. Visitation
4. Random and haphazard
5. Imposed and authoritarian
6. One person usually

MODERN
1. Study and analysis
2. Focused on aims, materials, methods, supervisors, employees, environment
3. Demonstrations, intervisitation, workshops, directed reading, bulletins, etc.
4. Definitely organized and planned (scientific)
5. Cooperative and democratic
6. Many persons involved (creative)

THE EIGHT (8) BASIC PRINCIPLES OF THE NEW SUPERVISION

I. Principle of Responsibility
   Authority to act and responsibility for acting must be joined.
   A. If you give responsibility, give authority.
   B. Define employee duties clearly.
   C. Protect employees from criticism by others.
   D. Recognize the rights as well as obligations of employees.
   E. Achieve the aims of a democratic society insofar as it is possible within the area of your work.
   F. Establish a situation favorable to training and learning.
   G. Accept ultimate responsibility for everything done in your section, unit, office, division, department.
   H. Good administration and good supervision are inseparable.

II. Principle of Authority
The success of the supervisor is measured by the extent to which the power of authority is not used.
   A. Exercise simplicity and informality in supervision
   B. Use the simplest machinery of supervision
   C. If it is good for the organization as a whole, it is probably justified.
   D. Seldom be arbitrary or authoritative.
   E. Do not base your work on the power of position or of personality.
   F. Permit and encourage the free expression of opinions.

III. Principle of Self-Growth
The success of the supervisor is measured by the extent to which, and the speed with which, he is no longer needed.
   A. Base criticism on principles, not on specifics.
   B. Point out higher activities to employees.
   C. Train for self-thinking by employees to meet new situations.
   D. Stimulate initiative, self-reliance, and individual responsibility
   E. Concentrate on stimulating the growth of employees rather than on removing defects.

IV. Principle of Individual Worth
Respect for the individual is a paramount consideration in supervision.
   A. Be human and sympathetic in dealing with employees.
   B. Don't nag about things to be done.
   C. Recognize the individual differences among employees and seek opportunities to permit best expression of each personality.

V. Principle of Creative Leadership
The best supervision is that which is not apparent to the employee.
   A. Stimulate, don't drive employees to creative action.
   B. Emphasize doing good things.
   C. Encourage employees to do what they do best.
   D. Do not be too greatly concerned with details of subject or method.
   E. Do not be concerned exclusively with immediate problems and activities.
   F. Reveal higher activities and make them both desired and maximally possible.
   G. Determine procedures in the light of each situation but see that these are derived from a sound basic philosophy.
   H. Aid, inspire, and lead so as to liberate the creative spirit latent in all good employees.

VI. Principle of Success and Failure
There are no unsuccessful employees, only unsuccessful supervisors who have failed to give proper leadership.
   A. Adapt suggestions to the capacities, attitudes, and prejudices of employees.
   B. Be gradual, be progressive, be persistent.
   C. Help the employee find the general principle; have the employee apply his own problem to the general principle.
   D. Give adequate appreciation for good work and honest effort.
   E. Anticipate employee difficulties and help to prevent them.
   F. Encourage employees to do the desirable things they will do anyway.
   G. Judge your supervision by the results it secures.

VII. Principle of Science
Successful supervision is scientific, objective, and experimental. It is based on facts, not on prejudices.
   A. Be cumulative in results.
   B. Never divorce your suggestions from the goals of training.
   C. Don't be impatient of results.
   D. Keep all matters on a professional, not a personal, level.
   E. Do not be concerned exclusively with immediate problems and activities.
   F. Use objective means of determining achievement and rating where possible.

VIII. Principle of Cooperation
Supervision is a cooperative enterprise between supervisor and employee.
   A. Begin with conditions as they are.
   B. Ask opinions of all involved when formulating policies.
   C. Organization is as good as its weakest link.
   D. Let employees help to determine policies and department programs.
   E. Be approachable and accessible—physically and mentally.
   F. Develop pleasant social relationships.

WHAT IS ADMINISTRATION

Administration is concerned with providing the environment, the material facilities, and the operational procedures that will promote the maximum growth and development of supervisors and employees. (Organization is an aspect and a concomitant of administration.)

There is no sharp line of demarcation between supervision and administration; these functions are intimately interrelated and, often, overlapping. They are complementary activities.

I. Practices Commonly Classed as "Supervisory"
   A. Conducting employees' conferences
   B. Visiting sections, units, offices, divisions, departments
   C. Arranging for demonstrations
   D. Examining plans
   E. Suggesting professional reading
   F. Interpreting bulletins
   G. Recommending in-service training courses
   H. Encouraging experimentation
   I. Appraising employee morale
   J. Providing for intervisitation

II. Practices Commonly Classified as "Administrative"
   A. Management of the office
   B. Arrangement of schedules for extra duties
   C. Assignment of rooms or areas
   D. Distribution of supplies
   E. Keeping records and reports
   F. Care of audio-visual materials
   G. Keeping inventory records
   H. Checking record cards and books

      I.   Programming special activities
      J.   Checking on the attendance and punctuality of employees

III. Practices Commonly Classified as Both "Supervisory" and "Administrative"
     A.   Program construction
     B.   Testing or evaluating outcomes
     C.   Personnel accounting
     D.   Ordering instructional materials

RESPONSIBILITIES OF THE SUPERVISOR

A person employed in a supervisory capacity must constantly be able to improve his own efficiency and ability. He represent the employer to the employees and only continuous self-examination can make him a capable supervisor.

Leadership and training are the supervisor's responsibility. An efficient working unit is one in which the employees work with the supervisor. It is his job to bring out the best in his employees. He must always be relaxed, courteous, and calm in his association with his employees. Their feelings are important, and a harsh attitude does not develop the most efficient employees.

COMPETENCES OF THE SUPERVISOR

    I.   Complete knowledge of the duties and responsibilities of his position.
    II.   To be able to organize a job, plan ahead, and carry through.
    III. To have self-confidence and initiative.
    IV. To be able to handle the unexpected situation and make quick decisions.
    V.   To be able to properly train subordinates in the positions they are best suited for.
    VI. To be able to keep good human relations among his subordinates.
    VII. To be able to keep good human relations between his subordinates and himself and to earn their respect and trust.

THE PROFESSIONAL SUPERVISOR-EMPLOYEE RELATIONSHIP

There are two kinds of efficiency: one kind is only apparent and is produced in organizations through the exercise of mere discipline; this is but a simulation of the second, or true, efficiency which springs from spontaneous cooperation. If you are a manager, no matter how great or small your responsibility, it is your job, in the final analysis, to create and develop this involuntary cooperation among the people whom you supervise. For, no matter how powerful a combination of money, machines, and materials a company may have, this is a dead and sterile thing without a team of willing, thinking, and articulate people to guide it.

The following 21 points are presented as indicative of the exemplary basic relationship that should exist between supervisor and employee:

1. Each person wants to be liked and respected by his fellow employee and wants to be treated with consideration and respect by his superior.
2. The most competent employee will make an error. However, in a unit where good relations exist between the supervisor and his employees, tenseness and fear do not exist. Thus, errors are not hidden or covered up, and the efficiency of a unit is not impaired.

3. Subordinates resent rules, regulations, or orders that are unreasonable or unexplained.
4. Subordinates are quick to resent unfairness, harshness, injustices, and favoritism.
5. An employee will accept responsibility if he knows that he will be complimented for a job well done, and not too harshly chastised for failure; that his supervisor will check the cause of the failure, and, if it was the supervisor's fault, he will assume the blame therefore. If it was the employee's fault, his supervisor will explain the correct method or means of handling the responsibility.
6. An employee wants to receive credit for a suggestion he has made, that is used. If a suggestion cannot be used, the employee is entitled to an explanation. The supervisor should not say "no" and close the subject.
7. Fear and worry slow up a worker's ability. Poor working environment can impair his physical and mental health. A good supervisor avoids forceful methods, threats, and arguments to get a job done.
8. A forceful supervisor is able to train his employees individually and as a team, and is able to motivate them in the proper channels.
9. A mature supervisor is able to properly evaluate his subordinates and to keep them happy and satisfied.
10. A sensitive supervisor will never patronize his subordinates.
11. A worthy supervisor will respect his employees' confidences.
12. Definite and clear-cut responsibilities should be assigned to each executive.
13. Responsibility should always be coupled with corresponding authority.
14. No change should be made in the scope or responsibilities of a position without a definite understanding to that effect on the part of all persons concerned.
15. No executive or employee, occupying a single position in the organization, should be subject to definite orders from more than one source.
16. Orders should never be given to subordinates over the head of a responsible executive. Rather than do this, the officer in question should be supplanted.
17. Criticisms of subordinates should, whoever possible, be made privately, and in no case should a subordinate be criticized in the presence of executives or employees of equal or lower rank.
18. No dispute or difference between executives or employees as to authority or responsibilities should be considered too trivial for prompt and careful adjudication.
19. Promotions, wage changes, and disciplinary action should always be approved by the executive immediately superior to the one directly responsible.
20. No executive or employee should ever be required, or expected, to be at the same time an assistant to, and critic of, another.
21. Any executive whose work is subject to regular inspection should, wherever practicable, be given the assistance and facilities necessary to enable him to maintain an independent check of the quality of his work.

MINI-TEXT IN SUPERVISION, ADMINISTRATION, MANAGEMENT, AND ORGANIZATION

I. Brief Highlights

Listed concisely and sequentially are major headings and important data in the field for quick recall and review.

A. Levels of Management
Any organization of some size has several levels of management. In terms of a ladder, the levels are:

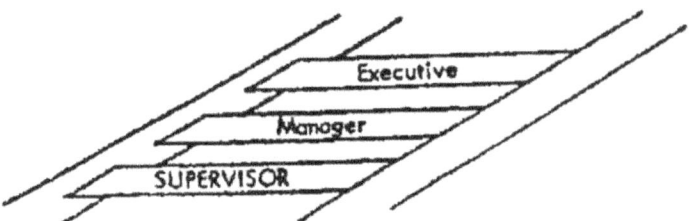

The first level is very important because it is the beginning point of management leadership.

B. What the Supervisor Must Learn
A supervisor must learn to:
1. Deal with people and their differences
2. Get the job done through people
3. Recognize the problems when they exist
4. Overcome obstacles to good performance
5. Evaluate the performance of people
6. Check his own performance in terms of accomplishment

C. A Definition of Supervisor
The term supervisor means any individual having authority, in the interests of the employer, to hire, transfer, suspend, lay-off, recall, promote, discharge, assign, reward, or discipline other employees or responsibility to direct them, or to adjust their grievances, or effectively to recommend such action, if, in connection with the foregoing, exercise of such authority is not of a merely routine or clerical nature but requires the use of independent judgment.

D. Elements of the Team Concept
What is involved in teamwork? The component parts are:
1. Members
2. A leader
3. Goals
4. Plans
5. Cooperation
6. Spirit

E. Principles of Organization
1. A team member must know what his job is.
2. Be sure that the nature and scope of a job are understood.
3. Authority and responsibility should be carefully spelled out.
4. A supervisor should be permitted to make the maximum number of decisions affecting his employees.
5. Employees should report to only one supervisor.
6. A supervisor should direct only as many employees as he can handle effectively.
7. An organization plan should be flexible.

8. Inspection and performance of work should be separate.
9. Organizational problems should receive immediate attention.
10. Assign work in line with ability and experience.

F. The Four Important Parts of Every Job
1. Inherent in every job is the *accountability* for results.
2. A second set of factors in every job is *responsibilities*.
3. Along with duties and responsibilities one must have the *authority* to act within certain limits without obtaining permission to proceed.
4. No job exists in a vacuum. The supervisor is surrounded by key *relationships*.

G. Principles of Delegation
Where work is delegated for the first time, the supervisor should think in terms of these questions:
1. Who is best qualified to do this?
2. Can an employee improve his abilities by doing this?
3. How long should an employee spend on this?
4. Are there any special problems for which he will need guidance?
5. How broad a delegation can I make?

H. Principles of Effective Communications
1. Determine the media.
2. To whom directed?
3. Identification and source authority.
4. Is communication understood?

I. Principles of Work Improvement
1. Most people usually do only the work which is assigned to them.
2. Workers are likely to fit assigned work into the time available to perform it.
3. A good workload usually stimulates output.
4. People usually do their best work when they know that results will be reviewed or inspected.
5. Employees usually feel that someone else is responsible for conditions of work, workplace layout, job methods, type of tools/equipment, and other such factors.
6. Employees are usually defensive about their job security.
7. Employees have natural resistance to change.
8. Employees can support or destroy a supervisor.
9. A supervisor usually earns the respect of his people through his personal example of diligence and efficiency.

J. Areas of Job Improvement
The areas of job improvement are quite numerous, but the most common ones which a supervisor can identify and utilize are:
1. Departmental layout
2. Flow of work
3. Workplace layout
4. Utilization of manpower
5. Work methods
6. Materials handling

7. Utilization
8. Motion economy

K. Seven Key Points in Making Improvements
1. Select the job to be improved
2. Study how it is being done now
3. Question the present method
4. Determine actions to be taken
5. Chart proposed method
6. Get approval and apply
7. Solicit worker participation

l. Corrective Techniques of Job Improvement
Specific Problems
1. Size of workload
2. Inability to meet schedules
3. Strain and fatigue
4. Improper use of men and skills
5. Waste, poor quality, unsafe conditions
6. Bottleneck conditions that hinder output
7. Poor utilization of equipment and machine
8. Efficiency and productivity of labor

General Improvement
1. Departmental layout
2. Flow of work
3. Work plan layout
4. Utilization of manpower
5. Work methods
6. Materials handling
7. Utilization of equipment
8. Motion economy

Corrective Techniques
1. Study with scale model
2. Flow chart study
3. Motion analysis
4. Comparison of units produced to standard allowance
5. Methods analysis
6. Flow chart and equipment study
7. Down time vs. running time
8. Motion analysis

M. A Planning Checklist
1. Objectives
2. Controls
3. Delegations
4. Communications
5. Resources
6. Manpower

7. Equipment
8. Supplies and materials
9. Utilization of time
10. Safety
11. Money
12. Work
13. Timing of improvements

N. Five Characteristics of Good Directions
In order to get results, directions must be:
1. Possible of accomplishment
2. Agreeable with worker interests
3. Related to mission
4. Planned and complete
5. Unmistakably clear

O. Types of Directions
1. Demands or direct orders
2. Requests
3. Suggestion or implication
4. volunteering

P. Controls
A typical listing of the overall areas in which the supervisor should establish controls might be:
1. Manpower
2. Materials
3. Quality of work
4. Quantity of work
5. Time
6. Space
7. Money
8. Methods

Q. Orienting the New Employee
1. Prepare for him
2. Welcome the new employee
3. Orientation for the job
4. Follow-up

R. Checklist for Orienting New Employees   Yes   No
1. Do you appreciate the feelings of new employees
   when they first report for work?   ___   ___
2. Are you aware of the fact that the new employee must
   make a big adjustment to his job?   ___   ___
3. Have you given him good reasons for liking the job and
   the organization?   ___   ___
4. Have you prepared for his first day on the job?   ___   ___
5. Did you welcome him cordially and make him feel needed?   ___   ___

			Yes	No
6.	Did you establish rapport with him so that he feels free to talk and discuss matters with you?		___	___
7.	Did you explain his job to him and his relationship to you?		___	___
8.	Does he know that his work will be evaluated periodically on a basis that is fair and objective?		___	___
9.	Did you introduce him to his fellow workers in such a way that they are likely to accept him?		___	___
10.	Does he know what employee benefits he will receive?		___	___
11.	Does he understand the importance of being on the job and what to do if he must leave his duty station?		___	___
12.	Has he been impressed with the importance of accident prevention and safe practice?		___	___
13.	Does he generally know his way around the department?		___	___
14.	Is he under the guidance of a sponsor who will teach the right way of doing things?		___	___
15.	Do you plan to follow-up so that he will continue to adjust successfully to his job?		___	___

S. Principles of Learning
1. Motivation
2. Demonstration or explanation
3. Practice

T. Causes of Poor Performance
1. Improper training for job
2. Wrong tools
3. Inadequate directions
4. Lack of supervisory follow-up
5. Poor communications
6. Lack of standards of performance
7. Wrong work habits
8. Low morale
9. Other

U. Four Major Steps in On-The-Job Instruction
1. Prepare the worker
2. Present the operation
3. Tryout performance
4. Follow-up

V. Employees Want Five Things
1. Security
2. Opportunity
3. Recognition
4. Inclusion
5. Expression

W. Some Don'ts in Regard to Praise
1. Don't praise a person for something he hasn't done.
2. Don't praise a person unless you can be sincere.
3. Don't be sparing in praise just because your superior withholds it from you.
4. Don't let too much time elapse between good performance and recognition of it

X. How to Gain Your Workers' Confidence
Methods of developing confidence include such things as:
1. Knowing the interests, habits, hobbies of employees
2. Admitting your own inadequacies
3. Sharing and telling of confidence in others
4. Supporting people when they are in trouble
5. Delegating matters that can be well handled
6. Being frank and straightforward about problems and working conditions
7. Encouraging others to bring their problems to you
8. Taking action on problems which impede worker progress

Y. Sources of Employee Problems
On-the-job causes might be such things as:
1. A feeling that favoritism is exercised in assignments
2. Assignment of overtime
3. An undue amount of supervision
4. Changing methods or systems
5. Stealing of ideas or trade secrets
6. Lack of interest in job
7. Threat of reduction in force
8. Ignorance or lack of communications
9. Poor equipment
10. Lack of knowing how supervisor feels toward employee
11. Shift assignments

Off-the-job problems might have to do with:
1. Health
2. Finances
3. Housing
4. Family

Z. The Supervisor's Key to Discipline
There are several key points about discipline which the supervisor should keep in mind:
1. Job discipline is one of the disciplines of life and is directed by the supervisor.
2. It is more important to correct an employee fault than to fix blame for it.
3. Employee performance is affected by problems both on the job and off.
4. Sudden or abrupt changes in behavior can be indications of important employee problems.
5. Problems should be dealt with as soon as possible after they are identified.
6. The attitude of the supervisor may have more to do with solving problems than the techniques of problem solving.
7. Correction of employee behavior should be resorted to only after the supervisor is sure that training or counseling will not be helpful.

8. Be sure to document your disciplinary actions.
9. Make sure that you are disciplining on the basis of facts rather than personal feelings.
10. Take each disciplinary step in order, being careful not to make snap judgments, or decisions based on impatience.

AA. Five Important Processes of Management
1. Planning
2. Organizing
3. Scheduling
4. Controlling
5. Motivating

BB. When the Supervisor Fails to Plan
1. Supervisor creates impression of not knowing his job
2. May lead to excessive overtime
3. Job runs itself—supervisor lacks control
4. Deadlines and appointments missed
5. Parts of the work go undone
6. Work interrupted by emergencies
7. Sets a bad example
8. Uneven workload creates peaks and valleys
9. Too much time on minor details at expense of more important tasks

CC. Fourteen General Principles of Management
1. Division of work
2. Authority and responsibility
3. Discipline
4. Unity of command
5. Unity of direction
6. Subordination of individual interest to general interest
7. Remuneration of personnel
8. Centralization
9. Scalar chain
10. Order
11. Equity
12. Stability of tenure of personnel
13. Initiative
14. Esprit de corps

DD. Change

Bringing about change is perhaps attempted more often, and yet less well understood, than anything else the supervisor does. How do people generally react to change? (People tend to resist change that is imposed upon them by other individuals or circumstances.

Change is characteristic of every situation. It is a part of every real endeavor where the efforts of people are concerned.

1. Why do people resist change?
   People may resist change because of:
   a. Fear of the unknown
   b. Implied criticism
   c. Unpleasant experiences in the past
   d. Fear of loss of status
   e. Threat to the ego
   f. Fear of loss of economic stability

2. How can we best overcome the resistance to change?
   In initiating change, take these steps:
   a. Get ready to sell
   b. Identify sources of help
   c. Anticipate objections
   d. Sell benefits
   e. Listen in depth
   f. Follow up

II. Brief Topical Summaries

   A. Who/What is the Supervisor?
      1. The supervisor is often called the "highest level employee and the lowest level manager."
      2. A supervisor is a member of both management and the work group. He acts as a bridge between the two.
      3. Most problems in supervision are in the area of human relations, or people problems.
      4. Employees expect: Respect, opportunity to learn and to advance, and a sense of belonging, and so forth.
      5. Supervisors are responsible for directing people and organizing work. Planning is of paramount importance.
      6. A position description is a set of duties and responsibilities inherent to a given position.
      7. It is important to keep the position description up-to-date and to provide each employee with his own copy.

   B. The Sociology of Work
      1. People are alike in many ways; however, each individual is unique.
      2. The supervisor is challenged in getting to know employee differences. Acquiring skills in evaluating individuals is an asset.
      3. Maintaining meaningful working relationships in the organization is of great importance.
      4. The supervisor has an obligation to help individuals to develop to their fullest potential.
      5. Job rotation on a planned basis helps to build versatility and to maintain interest and enthusiasm in work groups.
      6. Cross training (job rotation) provides backup skills.

7. The supervisor can help reduce tension by maintaining a sense of humor, providing guidance to employees, and by making reasonable and timely decisions. Employees respond favorably to working under reasonably predictable circumstances.
8. Change is characteristic of all managerial behavior. The supervisor must adjust to changes in procedures, new methods, technological changes, and to a number of new and sometimes challenging situations.
9. To overcome the natural tendency for people to resist change, the supervisor should become more skillful in initiating change.

C. Principles and Practices of Supervision
1. Employees should be required to answer to only one superior.
2. A supervisor can effectively direct only a limited number of employees, depending upon the complexity, variety, and proximity of the jobs involved.
3. The organizational chart presents the organization in graphic form. It reflects lines of authority and responsibility as well as interrelationships of units within the organization.
4. Distribution of work can be improved through an analysis using the "Work Distribution Chart."
5. The "Work Distribution Chart" reflects the division of work within a unit in understandable form.
6. When related tasks are given to an employee, he has a better chance of increasing his skills through training.
7. The individual who is given the responsibility for tasks must also be given the appropriate authority to insure adequate results.
8. The supervisor should delegate repetitive, routine work. Preparation of recurring reports, maintaining leave and attendance records are some examples.
9. Good discipline is essential to good task performance. Discipline is reflected in the actions of employees on the job in the absence of supervision.
10. Disciplinary action may have to be taken when the positive aspects of discipline have failed. Reprimand, warning, and suspension are examples of disciplinary action.
11. If a situation calls for a reprimand, be sure it is deserved and remember it is to be done in private.

D. Dynamic Leadership
1. A style is a personal method or manner of exerting influence.
2. Authoritarian leaders often see themselves as the source of power and authority.
3. The democratic leader often perceives the group as the source of authority and power.
4. Supervisors tend to do better when using the pattern of leadership that is most natural for them.
5. Social scientists suggest that the effective supervisor use the leadership style that best fits the problem or circumstances involved.
6. All four styles—telling, selling, consulting, joining—have their place. Using one does not preclude using the other at another time.

7. The theory X point of view assumes that the average person dislikes work, will avoid it whenever possible, and must be coerced to achieve organizational objectives.
8. The theory Y point of view assumes that the average person considers work to be a natural as play, and, when the individual is committed, he requires little supervision or direction to accomplish desired objectives.
9. The leader's basic assumptions concerning human behavior and human nature affect his actions, decisions, and other managerial practices.
10. Dissatisfaction among employees is often present, but difficult to isolate. The supervisor should seek to weaken dissatisfaction by keeping promises, being sincere and considerate, keeping employees informed, and so forth.
11. Constructive suggestions should be encouraged during the natural progress of the work.

E. Processes for Solving Problems
1. People find their daily tasks more meaningful and satisfying when they can improve them.
2. The causes of problems, or the key factors, are often hidden in the background. Ability to solve problems often involves the ability to isolate them from their backgrounds. There is some substance to the cliché that some persons "can't see the forest for the trees."
3. New procedures are often developed from old ones. Problems should be broken down into manageable parts. New ideas can be adapted from old one.
4. People think differently in problem-solving situations. Using a logical, patterned approach is often useful. One approach found to be useful includes these steps:
   a. Define the problem
   b. Establish objectives
   c. Get the facts
   d. Weigh and decide
   e. Take action
   f. Evaluate action

F. Training for Results
1. Participants respond best when they feel training is important to them.
2. The supervisor has responsibility for the training and development of those who report to him.
3. When training is delegated to others, great care must be exercised to insure the trainer has knowledge, aptitude, and interest for his work as a trainer.
4. Training (learning) of some type goes on continually. The most successful supervisor makes certain the learning contributes in a productive manner to operational goals.
5. New employees are particularly susceptible to training. Older employees facing new job situations require specific training, as well as having need for development and growth opportunities.
6. Training needs require continuous monitoring.
7. The training officer of an agency is a professional with a responsibility to assist supervisors in solving training problems.

8. Many of the self-development steps important to the supervisor's own growth are equally important to the development of peers and subordinates. Knowledge of these is important when the supervisor consults with others on development and growth opportunities.

G. Health, Safety, and Accident Prevention
1. Management-minded supervisors take appropriate measures to assist employees in maintaining health and in assuring safe practices in the work environment.
2. Effective safety training and practices help to avoid injury and accidents.
3. Safety should be a management goal. All infractions of safety which are observed should be corrected without exception.
4. Employees' safety attitude, training and instruction, provision of safe tools and equipment, supervision, and leadership are considered highly important factors which contribute to safety and which can be influenced directly by supervisors.
5. When accidents do occur, they should be investigated promptly for very important reasons, including the fact that information which is gained can be used to prevent accidents in the future.

H. Equal Employment Opportunity
1. The supervisor should endeavor to treat all employees fairly, without regard to religion, race, sex, or national origin.
2. Groups tend to reflect the attitude of the leader. Prejudice can be detected even in very subtle form. Supervisors must strive to create a feeling of mutual respect and confidence in every employee.
3. Complete utilization of all human resources is a national goal. Equitable consideration should be accorded women in the work force, minority-group members, the physically and mentally handicapped, and the older employee. The important question is: "Who can do the job?"
4. Training opportunities, recognition for performance, overtime assignments, promotional opportunities, and all other personnel actions are to be handled on an equitable basis.

I. Improving Communications
1. Communications is achieving understanding between the sender and the receiver of a message. It also means sharing information—the creation of understanding.
2. Communication is basic to all human activity. Words are means of conveying meanings; however, real meanings are in people.
3. There are very practical differences in the effectiveness of one-way, impersonal, and two-way communications. Words spoken face-to-face are better understood. Telephone conversations are effective, but lack the rapport of person-to-person exchanges. The whole person communicates.
4. Cooperation and communication in an organization go hand in hand. When there is a mutual respect between people, spelling out rules and procedures for communicating is unnecessary.
5. There are several barriers to effective communications. These include failure to listen with respect and understanding, lack of skill in feedback, and misinterpreting the meanings of words used by the speaker. It is also common

practice to listen to what we want to hear, and tune out things we do not want to hear.
6. Communication is management's chief problem. The supervisor should accept the challenge to communicate more effectively and to improve interagency and intra-agency communications.
7. The supervisor may often plan for and conduct meetings. The planning phase is critical and may determine the success or the failure of a meeting.
8. Speaking before groups usually requires extra effort. Stage fright may never disappear completely, but it can be controlled.

J. Self-Development
1. Every employee is responsible for his own self-development.
2. Toastmaster and toastmistress clubs offer opportunities to improve skills in oral communications.
3. Planning for one's own self-development is of vital importance. Supervisors know their own strengths and limitations better than anyone else.
4. Many opportunities are open to aid the supervisor in his developmental efforts, including job assignments; training opportunities, both governmental and non-governmental—to include universities and professional conferences and seminars.
5. Programmed instruction offers a means of studying at one's own rate.
6. Where difficulties may arise from a supervisor's being away from his work for training, he may participate in televised home study or correspondence courses to meet his self-development needs.

K. Teaching and Training
1. The Teaching Process
Teaching is encouraging and guiding the learning activities of students toward established goals. In most cases this process consists of five steps: preparation, presentation, summarization, evaluation, and application.

   a. Preparation
   Preparation is two-fold in nature; that of the supervisor and the employee. Preparation by the supervisor is absolutely essential to success. He must know what, when, where, how, and whom he will teach. Some of the factors that should be considered are:
   1) The objectives
   2) The materials needed
   3) The methods to be used
   4) Employee participation
   5) Employee interest
   6) Training aids
   7) Evaluation
   8) Summarization

   Employee preparation consists in preparing the employee to receive the material. Probably the most important single factor in the preparation of the employee is arousing and maintaining his interest. He must know the objectives of the training, why he is there, how the material can be used, and its importance to him.

b. Presentation
In presentation, have a carefully designed plan and follow it. The plan should be accurate and complete, yet flexible enough to meet situations as they arise. The method of presentation will be determined by the particular situation and objectives.

c. Summary
A summary should be made at the end of every training unit and program. In addition, there may be internal summaries depending on the nature of the material being taught. The important thing is that the trainee must always be able to understand how each part of the new material relates to the whole.

d. Application
The supervisor must arrange work so the employee will be given a chance to apply new knowledge or skills while the material is still clear in his mind and interest is high. The trainee does not really know whether he has learned the material until he has been given a chance to apply it. If the material is not applied, it loses most of its value.

e. Evaluation
The purpose of all training is to promote learning. To determine whether the training has been a success or failure, the supervisor must evaluate this learning.
In the broadest sense, evaluation includes all the devices, methods, skills, and techniques used by the supervisor to keep himself and the employees informed as to their progress toward the objectives they are pursuing. The extent to which the employee has mastered the knowledge, skills, and abilities, or changed his attitudes, as determined by the program objectives, is the extent to which instruction has succeeded or failed.
Evaluation should not be confined to the end of the lesson, day, or program but should be used continuously. We shall note later the way this relates to the rest of the teaching process.

2. Teaching Methods
A teaching method is a pattern of identifiable student and instructor activity used in presenting training material.
All supervisors are faced with the problem of deciding which method should be used at a given time.

a. Lecture
The lecture is direct oral presentation of material by the supervisor. The present trend is to place less emphasis on the trainer's activity and more on that of the trainee.

b. Discussion
Teaching by discussion or conference involves using questions and other techniques to arouse interest and focus attention upon certain areas, and by doing so creating a learning situation. This can be one of the most

valuable methods because it gives the employees an opportunity to express their ideas and pool their knowledge.

    c. Demonstration
The demonstration is used to teach how something works or how to do something. It can be used to show a principle or what the results of a series of actions will be. A well-staged demonstration is particularly effective because it shows proper methods of performance in a realistic manner.

    d. Performance
Performance is one of the most fundamental of all learning techniques or teaching methods. The trainee may be able to tell how a specific operation should be performed but he cannot be sure he knows how to perform the operation until he has done so.
As with all methods, there are certain advantages and disadvantages to each method.

    e. Which Method to Use
Moreover, there are other methods and techniques of teaching. It is difficult to use any method without other methods entering into it. In any learning situation, a combination of methods is usually more effective than any one method alone.

Finally, evaluation must be integrated into the other aspects of the teaching-learning process.

It must be used in the motivation of the trainees; it must be used to assist in developing understanding during the training; and it must be related to employee application of the results of training.

This is distinctly the role of the supervisor.

TRAINING PRINCIPLES AND PRACTICES

INTRODUCTION

1. Objective of Training — The WHY

   The purpose of training is to improve knowledge, skills, attitudes, and habits of employees so that they may better perform their assignments.

   Training needs can be defined on the basis of what the employee can do versus what he is required to do.

2. Time of Training Session — The WHEN

   Training needs can be identified from a study of existing records, such as turnover, absenteeism, grievances, production, waste of materials, number of *unsatisfactory* ratings, and accidents. Periodic surveys and interviews held with top level staff and line officials may locate areas in which training can help improve the operating services.

3. Space to be used to Conduct Session — The WHERE

   Availability of adequate space, free from noise and interruption; good ventilation and light.

4. Determine Teaching Method — The HOW

   a. Conference Technique. This is recognized as the most effective method for developing and improving proper work attitudes.
   b. Lecture Method. Use this method only where necessary information could not be obtained from the group.
   c. Role Play. Provides a learning experience by acting out situations found on the job.
   d. Field Trips Where Applicable.
   e. Case Studies. Review a case study as an aid in problem-solving.

5. Use of Training Aids — The WHAT

   a. Audiovisual
   b. Printed material, etc.

6. Use of Experts on Phases of Training — The WHO

   Good policy to select instructors from among the operating staff who have the capability and experience through training to assure effective presentation of subject matter.

Necessary Clearances from Top Management. Obtain management and employee support. A good relationship with all operating officials must prevail if they are to be encouraged to use the services that are available to them. Training staff to assist line must understand the special problems line is encountering.

Evaluate Program

> Supervisors can check results by comparing past with present performance, attitudes and skills. Trainees opinions should be considered.
>
> Did the Program accomplish its purpose?

LESSON PLAN — TRAINING

OBJECTIVES: The purpose of training is to improve skill, improve work habits, improve attitude and increase productivity.

It is the job of the supervisor to see that employees under his supervision are properly trained to do the job that is expected of them. The actual training may be done by the supervisor or may be delegated to a capable, experienced employee.

ADVANTAGES TO A SUPERVISOR OF HAVING A WELL-TRAINED STAFF

1. Gives supervisor time to devote to planning better supervision.
2. Permits supervisor time to train new and retrain old employees.
3. Promotes initiative.
4. Work can be carried on in absence of supervisor.
5. Increases prestige of supervisor in eyes of management.
6. Fewer accidents.
7. Employees have more confidence in themselves, resulting in higher morale.
8. Less damage to equipment.

PRINCIPLES OF LEARNING

1. Individuals must be receptive for maximum learning.
2. Individuals must be motivated and interested.
3. We learn by repetition.
4. We learn one thing at a time.
5. Instructions must be made simple and broken down to essentials.
6. We tie our new learning to what we already know.
7. Individual differences — We differ from one another in ability and background. We learn at different rates of speed.
8. Concentration and participation by employees are required for effective learning.
9. We learn better when there is continuity of thought — when one step logically follows another.
10. We learn better and faster when we realize we are making progress.
11. A competitive spirit speeds up learning.
12. The employee learns better when he has confidence in his ability to learn.
13. We learn through senses: What we know comes through the sense of:
    Sight - 75%; Hearing - 13%; Touch - 6%; Smell - 3%; Taste - 3%.
14. We must understand what we learn to use our learning effectivity.

FOUR-STEP APPROACH TO TRAINING

1. Preparation.
2. Presentation.
3. Try-out performance by learner.
4. Follow-up.
   a. Preparation: Considered from viewpoint of:
      (1) The instructor
      (2) The learner
      (3) The job
      (4) The facilities

      (a) The instructor - should prepare himself by deciding: The best way to do the job.
      The method to be used in instruction.
      The amount of instruction to give at each session.
      The teaching materials necessary and available.
      (b) The learner - should be prepared by: Being at ease.
      Finding out what he already knows about the job. Getting him interested in learning the job.
      (c) The job - should be analyzed completely, broken down to its component units, key points in each operation stressed.
      (d) The facilities - should be adequate and conducive to learning, such as:
      Adequate space, lighting, ventilation and visual aids. No distracting influences.

   b. Presentation:
      (1) Tell, show, illustrate and question carefully and patiently.
      (2) Stress key points
      (3) Illustrate clearly and completely, taking up one point at a time, but no more than he can master.

   c. Try-Out Performance by Learner. (Self-explanatory)

   d. Follow-up:
      (1) Put him on his own.
      (2) Designate to whom he goes for help.
      (3) Check frequently — encourage questions.
      (4) Get him to look for key points as he progresses.
      (5) Taper off extra coaching.

CONCLUSION: If the learner hasn't learned, the instructor hasn't taught.

SENSITIVITY TRAINING

The goal of *sensitivity training* is to make employees more sensitive to themselves and to others, to make them aware of how, consciously and unconsciously, they affect others and others influence them. A manager will do a better job of achieving results through the efforts of others if he has this heightened sensitivity to others. The sensitivity training situation is designed to bring to the surface, for conscious examination, the normally unquestioned assumptions regarding role behavior, spheres of authority and worker relationships. The characteristics of the sensitivity training situation include:

- No formal authority or status is recognized in the group.
- No agenda is established.
- No goal for the group to work toward is created.
- No prescribed way for the group to reach decisions is established.
- No instruction to participants is given by the instructor or *trainer*.
- Whatever the group wants to discuss is followed.

There are several disadvantages to sensitivity training. It is time-consuming, and often requires the group to live together for a period of time (usually 2 to 3 weeks). It may be unpleasant to certain individuals in the early stages of group discussions. However, almost all of the organizations that have used it have found it to be an effective method of promoting greater understanding of how groups operate and how individuals function in them.

SUPERVISOR'S CHECK LIST FOR ORIENTATION

1. Prepare to receive the new employee.

   a. Arrange for a private interview, if possible, if not it should at least be uninterrupted. Be prepared to give the new employee your undivided attention.
   b. Review his work experience, education and training.
   c. Have an up-to-date description of his job available for discussion.
   d. Have his work place, equipment and supplies ready.

2. Welcome the new employee.

   a. Welcome the new employee and call her by name.
   b. Indicate your relationship to the new employee.
   c. Make her feel wanted, that you consider her a valuable addition to your team; that her abilities and cooperation are needed to get the job done.
   d. Give her a feeling of confidence in herself. Tell her you have no doubt she will learn easily and that she will adjust readily to her new job.

3. Show genuine interest in the employee.

   a. Discuss his background and interests.
   b. Inquire about his transportation to and from work.

4. Explain facts about her job.

   a. Explain the specific functions of the unit.
   b. Explain her duties and responsibilities.
   c. Make clear what will be expected of her.
   d. Encourage her to ask questions.

e. Show how her work is related to the work of others in the unit and how it fits into the work of the Department as a whole.
   f. Explain lines of authority.
   g. Explain to whom to go for help.

5. Sell the new employee on his job.

   a. Discuss with him the job advantages (friendly atmosphere, pleasant surroundings, security, promotion, pension, social security, municipal credit union, blood bank, grievance machinery and rewards for suggestions.)
   b. Sell him on his Department.
   c. Bring out the importance of his job in relation to the work of the unit and the Department as a whole.

6. Show employee the layout and facilities.

   a. Explain layout of unit or office.
   b. Show him facilities such as elevators, wash room, locker, etc.

7. Introduce him to co-workers.

   a. Indicate to each the new employee's duties.
   b. Explain duties of each person to whom introduced.
   c. Introduce to a well-qualified and trained sponsor who will go to lunch with the new employee and who will be available to answer questions.

8. Explain rules and regulations.

   a. Hours of work.
   b. Punctuality and attendance - signing in and out.
   c. Lunch period.
   d. Rest period.
   e. Use of telephone.
   f. Leave rules as administered.
   g. Other shop and office practices; smoking, safety regulations; safety program.
   h. Wearing of uniform, if required.
   i. Probationary period.
   j. Importance of good public relations.

9. Provide for job instruction

   Supervisor may instruct the new employee, or he may delegate this responsibility to a competent subordinate.

10. Follow-Up.

    a. Follow-up to see how new employee is progressing.
    b. Toward the end of the first day, show your personal interest by asking him how he is getting along or by encouraging him to ask questions, and by letting him know you want to be helpful.
    c. Make provision for frequent conferences with the new employee during the initial period of his employment.
    d. Keep the new employee posted on the progress he is making.

e. Continue to exercise close supervision with gradual tapering off as the employee demonstrates less need for close supervision.

SYSTEMS OF DIVIDING WORK AMONG EMPLOYEES

1. Series (or assembly-line)

    a. The assembly line approach, where each worker performs part of a job. For example, in an operation for collecting license fees, one employee checks the form, another collects the fees, and a third issues the receipt.
    b. Example - Sanitation, one worker loads, another drives truck.
    c. Advantages:
        (1) Short training for individual jobs which are relatively simple.
        (2) Greater availability of workers for simpler jobs when skilled labor market is tight.
        (3) Full use of highest skills of experienced employees on work requiring their skill.
    d. Disadvantages:
        (1) Added transportation and cycle time.
        (2) Reduced worker interest.
        (3) Added *comprehension* time.
        (4) Inflexibility of work force (inability to shift workers from one job to another to meet changing needs.)

2. Parallel

    a. A number of employees, each performing the complete job.
    b. Each worker checks form, collects fees, and issues receipt.
    c. Advantages:
        (1) Flexibility of work force.
        (2) Reduced comprehension time.
        (3) Reduced transportation of work item.
        (4) High worker interest.
    d. Disadvantages:
        (1) Increased training time.
        (2) Limited availability of higher skilled persons in employment market.
        (3) Use of some time of skilled workers on jobs not requiring highest skill.

3. Unit-assembly (simultaneous handling)

    a. Description - A number of operations are combined into a un:.t. Each worker on a team completes a different unit. Several teams are in operation.
    b. Advantages:
        (1) Same as those of serial plan.
        (2) Minimizes cycle-time.
    c. Disadvantages:
        (1) Same as those of serial plan, except for long cycle-time.
        (2) Can only be supplied in limited situations, where work 1 can be treated in separate parts.
        (3) Requires the addition of whatever steps are necessary to separate, route and reassemble work item.

4. Combination systems -- all possible combinations of serial, parallel and unit-assembly plans.

www.ingramcontent.com/pod-product-compliance
Lightning Source LLC
Chambersburg PA
CBHW081829300426
44116CB00014B/2521